16000 Lancaster Highway
Charlotte, NC 28277-2061

THE PROPHETIC MINISTRY

RICK JOYNER

MorningStar
PUBLICATIONS

16000 Lancaster Highway
Charlotte, NC 28277-2061

The Prophetic Ministry

by Rick Joyner

Printed in the United States of America.

International Standard Book Number 1-878327-62-3.

MorningStar Publications & Ministries
16000 Lancaster Highway
Charlotte, NC 28277

MorningStar's Website: http://www.eaglestar.org

For information call 704-542-0278.

This book is dedicated to Paul Cain and Bob Jones. Though these two men are very different from one another, each in his own way has been a spiritual father to me, and to thousands of other emerging prophetic ministries around the world. Not only have they demonstrated prophetic gifts of biblical stature, they have done so in such love, integrity and humility that the prophetic ministry is again taking its rightful place in the body of Christ.

PART
I

The Foundation

What is a prophet? What is prophecy? Who is to prophesy? How do the prophetic gifts and ministries function in the local church? To whom should a prophet be accountable? Since we have the Bible for guidance, why do we need prophecy? If all God's people are able to hear His voice, why do we need prophets? Is it right to seek prophecy? These are just a few of the common questions being asked today. If the church does not give the right answers to these questions, we can be sure that the vacuum created by ignorance will be filled with many erroneous views and dangerous practices.

In both the church and the world, there is a new hunger for the prophetic. This hunger stems from an increasing desire for guidance in order to survive the rampant confusion of our times. However, the need for guidance is not new among God's people. In fact, prophecy was a primary way through which the Lord related to His people in both the Old and New Testaments.

Humility to receive the Lord's guidance through others is a characteristic of those whom the Lord trusts with spiritual authority. King David, one of the greatest biblical prophets, wrote Scripture and is the subject of large sections of the Bible. Yet, in humility, he frequently called for the prophets when he needed personal guidance. As long as he lived, he heeded their words to him and remained open to their influence.

Another reason why there is such an increase of interest in this subject is because prophetic ministries and gifts of true biblical stature are being restored to the church today. This is a present-day fulfillment of Joel's prophecy, quoted by Peter on the day of Pentecost:

> **And it shall come to pass in the last days, saith God, I will pour out of my Spirit upon all flesh: and your sons and your daughters shall prophesy, and your young men shall see visions, and your old men shall dream dreams:**
>
> **And on my servants and on my handmaidens I will pour out in those days of my Spirit;** *and they shall prophesy* **(Acts 2:17-18 KJV).**

This passage indicates that there will be a dramatic increase in prophecy, dreams and visions in the last days. As we draw near to the end of this age, we will frequently need specific and accurate guidance. Because wars, natural disasters and persecutions are such a pervasive part of the end-time scenario, the church will experience an increasing need for prophetic foresight.

Prophetic ministry in the last days will parallel New Testament examples such as Agabus, who foresaw a worldwide famine (see Acts 11:28), and Paul, who went to Macedonia at the right time in response to a prophetic dream (see Acts 16:9-10). Prophetic revelation will enable the church to prepare for future needs and will dramatically increase the success of our missionary outreach.

Counterfeit Prophetic Ministry

Along with the restoration of legitimate prophetic ministry, there is a corresponding increase of false prophecy and false prophets. False prophets have real power and must be recognized if we are to avoid becoming their prey. The desperate hunger for supernatural guidance has spawned entire television networks devoted to psychic revelation. Just as Moses' God-given power greatly exceeded the demonic power of Pharaoh's sorcerers, the Lord's prophetic gifts to His church greatly exceed anything offered by psychics.

There are sound biblical answers to the questions now being raised about the prophetic, and it is crucial that we understand and address them. The Scriptures indicate that this will be one of the most important issues at the end of this age. Those who try to avoid the issue of the prophetic by pretending that it does not exist will become increasingly subject to the enemy's schemes. The Lord has given us every provision we need to accomplish His purposes and prevail over the enemy, and we would be foolish to reject any of the resources that He provides. As the apostle Paul said concerning his own ministry:

> **And my message and my preaching were not in persuasive words of wisdom, but in demonstration of the Spirit and of power,**
>
> **that your faith should not rest on the wisdom of men, but on the power of God (I Corinthians 2:4-5).**
>
> **For our gospel did not come to you in word only, but also in power and in the Holy Spirit and with full conviction; just as you know what kind of men we proved to be among you for your sake (I Thessalonians 1:5).**

The truth of God is the greatest force on earth, but Paul understood that his message must be characterized by supernatural power rather than by words alone. This was also true of the Lord Jesus Himself. He *was* the Truth, but He still used the power of miracles to confirm His message. If this was true of the Lord Jesus and the apostles, how much more do we need to have His power confirming *our* words?

Even if we are not called to the office of a prophet, we need to understand this ministry. The entire church is called as a prophetic voice to the nations. Together we are to serve as the Lord's spokesmen to the world. The prophetic ministry is listed as one of the primary ministries given **"for the equipping of the saints for the work of service" (Ephesians 4:12).** The prophetic gifts are not just an optional novelty for the super-spiritual; they are essential tools for effective functioning in pastoral, teaching, evangelistic or apostolic ministry.

For example, effectively using words of knowledge can reduce to a fraction the time many pastors spend in counseling sessions. An evangelist using that gift can speak to one woman and stir an entire city, just as Jesus did with the woman at the well. The gifts of the Spirit are not toys but tools. The Lord gives prophetic gifts because we need them, not for our entertainment. When used correctly, they will multiply the spiritual effectiveness of any ministry. This is why the apostle Paul exhorted the church, **"Desire earnestly spiritual gifts, but especially that you may prophesy" (I Corinthians 14:1).**

17

Questions Regarding the Prophetic

We must understand how to properly use the gifts entrusted to us. This includes becoming aware of the traps which the enemy sets for all who walk in the supernatural realm. Leaders who are called to equip the emerging prophetic ministries must also understand these matters. This book will address such questions as:

- Why do we need prophets today?

- How does current prophetic revelation relate to the revelation contained in the Scriptures?

- How do New Covenant prophets differ from their Old Covenant counterparts?

- How does the prophet relate to and function in the local church?

- Can a true prophet give an inaccurate prediction?

- Why does the Lord speak through dreams and visions instead of just telling us plainly?

- How are we to interpret supernatural revelations, dreams and visions?

- How does one function in the revelation gifts of the Spirit such as prophecy, the word of knowledge, the word of wisdom, and discernment of spirits?

- What are the characteristics of the counterfeit gifts of the Spirit, and how can we recognize them?

My goal in addressing these questions is to be both biblical and practical. We must be biblical if we are going to establish the real and recognize the false. We want to be practical in order to aid the effective release of true prophetic gifts and ministries in the church. This study will deal primarily with foundational issues pertaining to the prophetic, but we will also build upon them with more advanced issues.

This book is not targeted only to those who are specifically called to the prophetic ministry. Every Christian should be able to both hear from the Lord and at times speak a specific word from Him. The general principles addressed in this book will apply in some degree to all Christians who desire to know the Lord's voice.

Many Christians have a genuine prophetic gift or call to prophetic ministry, yet have been discouraged from pursuing their calling because of past mistakes. As I was shown years ago, the first part of the harvest will be the recovery and restoration of such ministries. My prayer is that this study will help stir up these gifts and give people the courage to rise again and pursue their purpose in the Lord.

It is also my desire to help those who have the gifts functioning in their lives, but who have not really understood them or known what to do with them. God wants to see the talents and spiritual gifts that He has entrusted to us used to bring a maximum return for His kingdom.

And finally, to those who have never been used by the Lord in one of the gifts of the Spirit, but have a genuine desire to, I pray that this study will help you in your quest so that you can be fully equipped for your place in God's plan.

TWO

Drawing From A Pure Well

Pure motives are crucial if we are going to function in true ministry. Living waters spring up from the **"innermost being" (John 7:38),** or the heart. Our motives accurately reveal what is in our heart. The more pure the heart, the purer the waters will be that come from it. Because a bad tree cannot bring forth good fruit, all who minister must **"watch over your heart with all diligence, for from it flow the springs of life" (Proverbs 4:23).** Because we are serving God's own children, we must offer them the purest of waters. For this reason the Lord Jesus said, **"For their sakes I sanctify Myself, that they themselves also may be sanctified in truth" (John 17:19).**

The apostle Paul exhorts us, **"Test yourselves to see if you are in the faith" (II Corinthians 13:5).** This test is primarily an examination and purification of our motives. The test is not complicated, but we must diligently apply it to ourselves if we are going to maintain purity of character and ministry before the Lord. One of the goals of this study is to illuminate this test so that we can properly examine ourselves and our ministries to be sure we are walking in obedience.

As we study spiritual gifts and ministries, it is right that we consider the importance of integrity and proper motives. Some of these lessons and insights will be purposely repeated in this book. Redundancy helps retention (see II Peter 1:12-13). Each time a principle is repeated and read with humility, there is a greater potential for it to be transferred from mere intellectual assent to true understanding and obedience of heart.

Believing in our *minds* is not what results in righteousness, but believing in our *hearts* (see Romans 10:10). **"God is opposed to the proud, but gives grace to the humble" (James 4:6). "Knowledge makes arrogant, but love edifies" (I Corinthians 8:1).** We are not merely seeking knowledge, but a love for the truth. When we hear something that we already know and humbly listen to what the Lord is saying, there is a grace released that brings the transfer of knowledge from our minds to our hearts. The goal is not to *know* but to *become*.

Closer to God

A closer walk with the Lord must be the basic motivation for all who seek prophetic gifts or ministry. Amos 3:7 declares, **"Surely the Lord GOD does nothing unless He reveals His secret counsel to His servants the prophets."** Nowhere does the Bible state that the Lord *must* do this. It is not a matter of legal obligation. Rather, the Lord does not *want* to do anything without sharing it with the prophets, because the prophets are His friends.

The true essence of prophetic ministry is to be so close to the Lord that He does not want to do anything without sharing it with you. There are special gifts and callings that are required of the prophetic ministry, but more than anything else, the essence of prophetic ministry is to be the special friend and confidant of the Lord. Therefore, friendship and intimacy with Him must always be our primary and ultimate goal.

The popular saying that we should "Seek the Giver and not the gifts" is not biblical. In fact, it is contrary to the scriptural exhortation to, **"Pursue love, yet *desire earnestly spiritual gifts*, but *especially* that you may prophesy"** **(I Corinthians 14:1).** We must pursue love first if our desire for spiritual gifts is to be pure, but this emphasis does not nullify the need to seek spiritual gifts.

Paul's statement that we should desire spiritual gifts is not just a suggestion—it is an apostolic command. We must never allow the gifts to supplant the Lord Himself as our preeminent quest, but it is impossible to get close to the ultimate Giver without receiving gifts. There are no gifts in this universe as precious as His spiritual gifts, and to receive them is evidence that we have found favor with the ultimate Giver.

Some people have determined to pursue love and then just stay open for the Lord to use them in spiritual gifts if He wants to—*but these people rarely get used!* We must **"earnestly desire"** spiritual gifts if we are going to receive them. But the only right reason to desire the gifts is for love's sake—in order to accomplish the purposes of the Lord and touch the needs of His people.

If we seek to be close to the Lord just to know what He is doing, we are using our relationship with Him in a tragically manipulative way. We must seek Him because we want to be close to Him, not because of what we can get from Him. What husband would be pleased if he knew that the only reason his wife wanted to be with him was to get information? The revelation of God's purposes will come if we seek to be close to Him, but it must never be our primary motive for doing so.

The Swirl of Controversy

The prophetic ministry and gifts have been a major source of attention in the church for over a decade now. There have been spectacular demonstrations of these gifts, having a positive effect on thousands of people. There has also been great controversy because of a few well-publicized mistakes by those who have prophetic gifts. Even when the prophetic gifts have been used properly, there have been misunderstandings.

The stringent standards applied to prophetic ministry are seldom applied to other ministries. Should we throw out the ministry of the pastor because some have made mistakes? Should we discard the ministry of evangelists or teachers because some have been dishonest or doctrinally defective? Of course not. In the same way, if we want to maintain the integrity of prophetic ministry, we must learn from the mistakes without throwing the baby out with the bath water.

During the late 1980s, the prophetic ministry captured the attention of the church on an almost unprecedented level. At that time, many prophetic ministers predicted that great controversy was coming to "purify the ranks," bring maturity to prophetic people, and support a more solid and effective advance that would come later. What has been called the "Prophetic Movement" has made some important advances, but there are obviously much greater movements to come. The prophetic ministry and gifts are destined to be thrust to the very forefront of issues facing the church worldwide, and they will ultimately help to ignite a spiritual advance that will have a positive impact on the entire church.

The Purposes of the Lord

The restoration of prophetic ministry to its biblical stature and integrity is important to the purposes of the Lord, but it is not the ultimate purpose of the Lord. It is part of the preparation for a much greater movement to come. Although the church will not be equipped for her mandate at the end of this age without the prophetic, this ministry is a means to an end, not an end in itself.

In order to avoid being carried away by another "wind of doctrine" or the latest Christian "flavor of the month," we must understand the Lord's greater purposes. As one friend of mine put it, "If we do not keep our attention focused on the ultimate purposes of the Lord, we will be continually distracted by the lesser purposes."

If the church is to accomplish her last-day ministry, she must have a prophetic ministry with trustworthy accuracy and impeccable integrity. We must know the Lord's plans before the time of their implementation so that we can properly position ourselves to carry them out.

A few prophetic ministries predicted years ahead of time that the walls were going to come down around the former communist states so that the gospel could be preached there for a period of time. Unfortunately, even those who knew these prophecies did not do much to actually prepare for it to happen. The church was basically caught off guard as one of the most profound watersheds in human history unfolded and shifted the political poles of the entire earth.

Tragically, many cults and spiritual fringe groups were more prepared for the changes in the former communist nations than the church, and they successfully rushed in to fill the vacuum of spiritual hunger in these countries. Will the same happen when China and Islamic countries become open to the gospel? And will the church continue to be caught off guard by the natural disasters and wars that create other great spiritual vacuums?

Almost a year before Hurricane Hugo struck my hometown of Charlotte, North Carolina, I was personally told by a prophet that "a great wind is going to come against your city, with rain blowing horizontally." A few months later this same person told me that he saw in a vision "a great demon rising up out of the sea to come against us in Charlotte." He said that this demon turned into a hurricane. Because a hurricane had never in history been able to sustain itself as far inland as Charlotte (200 miles), I speculated that this was a *"spiritual* hurricane."

Soon after that, I received a personal word from the Lord to buy camping equipment. I intended to do so, but procrastinated. A few months later, Hurricane Hugo slammed into Charlotte with full hurricane force. Watching the rain blowing horizontally as I looked out the window that night, I knew I had been very foolish not to seek the Lord for more clarity about this revelation. Power was knocked out in parts of the city for a month, and I was very sorry about my failure to buy the camping equipment.

Later, this same prophet told us there was going to be an earthquake in northern California in the coming fall. He said the center of the earthquake would be located just south of San Francisco, and stated specifically that the Oakland Bridge would not be safe. He predicted that the earthquake would register about "7" on the Richter scale, reflecting the level of shaking (spiritual, political and economic upheaval) that would soon come upon the world.

He also made a curious statement that this quake would be witnessed worldwide. None of us who heard his prophecy could imagine how such an event could be "witnessed worldwide." Yet the quake came just as we were told. It happened during the first game of the World Series at

Candlestick Park in San Francisco, and was broadcast live around the world.

Weeks before it happened, this same prophetic friend told me about the great snow storm of 1993 that came to the Carolinas and the Northeast. He added that it would come in the spring, on a date later than anything like this had happened before. On another occasion he told us about the floods coming to the Mississippi River and the Midwest weeks before they occurred.

I have never known this brother to miss anything that he has received in a dream or an open vision. We who know him have less than a perfect score in *interpreting* the revelations he shares with us, but we are learning. We are learning from many who are receiving revelation specifically and accurately about coming spiritual, political, economic and natural events. If the church is going to move with the kind of strategy and vision that the times demand, we must know how to receive, interpret and judge prophetic revelation.

What About Mistakes?

Mistakes are inevitable as we grow in the prophetic. When mistakes happen, we must be candid about them, with the hope that many can learn from our blunders and avoid having to make the same ones. Most of the prophetic men and women I associate with do not claim to be "prophets," nor do they care for such titles. They are simply trying to learn to hear from God accurately, and are devoted to seeing the whole church brought to the place where everyone can do the same.

Some believers hold to the teaching that a true prophet cannot make a mistake, and are offended by my mention of mistakes made by prophetic people. While I hope there will ultimately be a prophetic ministry raised up in the church with 100% accuracy, at the present time the only people I know who may claim 100% accuracy have never made a significant prediction worthy of a prophet. Though I may not personally ever reach a level of 100% accuracy on significant, detailed predictions—and therefore not merit the title "prophet" in the eyes of some—I intend to do all I can to make the way easier for others to attain that level.

Our goal should always be 100% accuracy in the reception, interpretation and application of prophetic revelation. While freely admitting that we are not there yet, we must pursue this goal without giving up until we get there. This will require being honest and straightforward with our mistakes, and humble with our successes. God gives His grace to the humble (James 4:6). We need to be far more concerned with walking in His grace than in receiving recognition for being prophetic.

THREE

Tares In The Wheat

Along with the extraordinary prophetic ministries now being released in the church, there is also a hoard of pseudo prophets circulating. This is to be expected. The Lord Himself warned us that every time He sows wheat, the enemy will try to sow tares in the same field. He also warned that in the last days **"many false prophets will arise, and will mislead many" (Matthew 24:11).** This warning that there will be many false prophets implies that there are also true ones. Otherwise, Jesus would have just said that *all* prophets in the last days will be false.

The only reason why there is counterfeit money is because there is also real money. There are no counterfeit three-dollar bills because there are no *real* three-dollar bills. As we will establish by the Scriptures, the prophetic ministry is given for the edification of the church and is to be included in the church's ministry until she is made perfect. To claim that we no longer need prophets is to claim that we are already perfect, which even the most casual observer would recognize as a major delusion.

Even so, we know that there are false prophets, and a lot of them! This includes false prophets who are in the church and those who are not. The falseness of those who are not in the church, such as cult leaders and those who are vehemently anti-Christ, is generally obvious. The enemy has a counterfeit for each of the true prophetic gifts, and they do have some power. The spiritual power being released by the New Age movement and other cult practices is real, but it is the supernatural power of the evil one. There are also false prophets and false spiritual gifts in the church. How can we discern the difference between the genuine and the false?

Many, out of a fear of deception, have shied away from all prophetic or other spiritual gifts. But if we allow the fear of deception to control us, we have already been deceived, and the enemy has accomplished his purpose. The church and the powers of evil are now moving swiftly toward the last- day confrontation foreseen by many of the prophets and apostles in Scripture. If we have not matured in our knowledge and use of the true gifts, we will be found tragically unprepared for this confrontation. Very soon, neutrality concerning spiritual gifts and power will not be possible. Those who have not matured in the use of true spiritual gifts will become increasingly subject to the false ones.

It would be impossible for the enemy to come and sow tares in the Lord's field if the Lord did not allow it. From this we must conclude that the Lord has purposes in the tares. One purpose is that He allows the enemy to sow tares in His field because learning to deal with the tares is helping to prepare us for the ultimate last-day confrontation.

The Lord knows the hearts of all men. He realized that Judas was a betrayer when He first chose him. He also knew that Judas was a thief, yet He gave him the money bag. Obviously there was something more important to the Lord than just keeping His money safe, or He would not have purposely given it to the one most inclined to pilfer it.

Right within His own inner circle, the Lord allowed people and situations to enter that would bring about a confrontation with evil. The training from this was far more important than perpetual harmony or the safekeeping of material goods. One of the Lord's primary strategies for preparing His disciples was to allow them to be confronted with the enemy from *within* the camp as well as outside.

Prematurely Uprooting the Tares

Many churches and ministries spend a considerable amount of effort trying to keep tares out of their field. This is a fruitless endeavor, because the Lord *wants* some of the tares to get in and He is going to let Satan continue to sow them. What was the Lord's wisdom for dealing with the tares? **"Allow both to grow *together* until the harvest" (Matthew 13:30).** He said that if we try to separate them before the harvest we will destroy the wheat along with the tares. Failing to understand this wisdom, many churches have destroyed the emerging young prophets and other ministries in their midst by prematurely trying to root out the tares.

Until **"the harvest,"** or the time of maturity, it is not really possible to tell the wheat from the tares. Tares actually look like wheat, but wheat is nutritious and tares are noxious. Fittingly, mature wheat bows over and tares remain standing upright. With maturity, the true gifts of God make one more humble. Counterfeit gifts will make one more proud.

Prior to the time of harvest, a prophet who is true, but immature, may be just as vain as a false prophet. Even one of the greatest prophets who ever lived, Samuel, tended to judge men by their external appearance rather than by the heart (see I Samuel 16). Some of the most discerning prophets I have ever met still have this same tendency. In fact, I have never met *anyone* who was completely free from this problem, including myself. It is not possible for us to truly know another person's heart except by revelation from the Lord—but that revelation is what we are seeking. We must learn to recognize one another after the spirit and not the flesh (II Corinthians 5:16).

When Jacob and Esau were young, most of us would have chosen the compliant, obedient Esau over the conniving, dishonest, schemer Jacob. But Esau had so little regard for the eternal inheritance in Christ that he was willing to sell his birthright for the immediate gratification of his flesh. Jacob was a liar, schemer and thief, but he loved the inheritance so much he was willing to jeopardize his own life to get it. Jacob was even willing to wrestle with an angel for the blessing. He recognized the surpassing value of the Lord's favor, and was willing to do whatever it took to obtain it. This pleased God far more than just being compliant.

Most true prophets, teachers, pastors, evangelists or apostles will have a "Jacob" nature until they have had the kind of encounter with God that Jacob experienced when he wrestled with Him. Many pastors and church leaders esteem peace and harmony in their congregations above the purposes of God. They would never say this, but their actions reveal it. Certainly we should value peace and unity, but not at the expense of the ultimate purposes of God. The only believers who are now in perfect order and harmony are in the cemetery!

As James Ryle once said, "All healthy living things grow; all growing things change; and change brings challenge."

Because of our tendency to put our security in our environment instead of in the Lord, most people, including most Christians, are very resistant to change. Change is unsettling if we have placed our confidence and security in our environment. This is actually one of the strongest yokes on human beings, and is the primary factor causing us to become old wineskins that are unable to receive new wine. This yoke is called "the tyranny of the familiar."

Trials and tribulations are often meant to help free us of this yoke so we will press further into the kingdom. We often need trials in order to keep us moving in the right direction. Conflict is not a sign that we are losing ground, but that ground is being taken. Which one of us would have chosen any of the disciples that the Lord chose? They seemed to cause Him as many problems as His enemies, and when He needed them most, they all deserted Him! It is apparent that we have much to learn about dealing both with the tares and the wheat.

The Treasures of Controversy

The church has experienced great controversy with the restoration of every truth and every one of the equipping ministries listed in Ephesians 4. Christendom was shaken when Martin Luther declared the priesthood of all believers, but he set the church on course for the restoration of the pastoral ministry. Wesley, Whitefield, Edwards and the others who helped to restore the ministry of the evangelist to the church were all accused of heresy and the most base forms of deception, immorality and corruption. Their accusers have long been forgotten, but the ministry they helped to restore to the church lives on. The same will be true of the prophetic and apostolic ministries.

The Lord allows controversy because it helps to purify the ministry He is raising up. First, controversy helps to correct the mistakes and extremes that inevitably come with the restoration of every truth and ministry. It also separates those who are seeking to identify with the new movement out of selfish ambition.

Controversy likewise helps to bring purity by removing the cowards. The Lord listed cowards along with unbelievers, the abominable, murderers, the immoral, sorcerers, idolaters and liars who will have their part in the lake of fire (see Revelation 21:8). Cowardice has no place in the kingdom of God, for true faith is characterized by courage. The Lord uses controversy and persecution as a means of separating the fearful and unbelieving from His work.

True Christianity, in Bible times and throughout church history, has normally existed amid controversy. It is a prophetic principle that often the natural realm reflects spiritual realities. Oil represents power. We anoint people with oil because oil represents the power of the Holy Spirit. It is no accident that the Middle East, the part of the world with the greatest oil reserves, is also the area that is embroiled in the greatest controversy. This is a reflection of a principle in the spiritual realm: The place of the greatest anointing is also going to be the place of the greatest conflict and controversy.

If we are not willing to fight for the Middle East oil, we will either lose the greatest source of power fueling our civilization, or become slaves to some of history's cruelest despots. The same is true of the anointing. The Lord often purposely situates what He is doing in a place of conflict and controversy, so that we must esteem His purposes above anything else in order to attain them.

We will never walk in the fullness of true ministry until we are willing to sacrifice everything but our love for the truth and God's will. To serve in ministry is the most holy and honorable commission that a person can have upon this earth. The Lord will not allow true ministry to be cheapened. But in order to keep it from being cheapened, He will allow its *appearance* to regularly be cheapened to remove pretension and separate those motivated by personal ambition.

It is likely that no other ministry carries the potential for either blessing or disaster as does the prophetic. But if we expect to have the wheat of a true prophetic ministry raised up in the church without any tares, the wheat will always elude us. Learning to deal with the tares is part of the curriculum. As Aleksandr Solzhenitsyn observed, "Even nature teaches us that perpetual well-being is not good for any living thing." Those who do not want any problems will not receive the blessings either.

If we trust the Lord to lead us into all truth more than we trust Satan to lead us into deception, we will be blessed with clear prophetic vision. This clarity of vision will be required if we are to accomplish our mandate for this hour, and in some cases, it will be necessary for our very survival. Prophetic ministry was given for the equipping of the church, and she will not be adequately prepared without it. Churches that do not **"[receive] a prophet in the name of a prophet" (Matthew 10:41)** will not receive the prophet's reward, or the benefit of the prophetic ministry.

The Responsibility of Speaking for God

Just as the church has a responsibility to open herself to the unfolding purposes of God, those who are called to the prophetic ministry have a responsibility to restore the essential integrity to this ministry. With the increased authority and anointing now being given to the prophetic office, there comes increased responsibility.

The definitions of the different Greek and Hebrew words translated "prophet" in the Old and New Testaments reveal that this ministry is one that speaks for God, has immediate intercourse with God, is an interpreter of the oracles of God, and preaches the counsel of God. These are all indicative of the awesome seriousness of prophetic ministry. To speak for God and interpret or preach His counsel is a responsibility of unfathomable proportions to be entrusted to mere men.

The Lord has magnified His word *above* even His name (Psalm 138:2). In biblical times, one's name was his identity. The same is still true, for we will be judged by our *words*, not our titles or reputations. To speak the Lord's words on His behalf must be considered one of the greatest responsibilities a person can have, and must be handled with the greatest of care and integrity.

When we start to be respected for our ministries and are given increasing influence in the church, our victories will yield greater fruit and our mistakes will do more damage. Although it is right to earnestly desire spiritual gifts, it is not only wrong, it will usually be tragic, when we seek visibility and influence prematurely. Those who really understand spiritual authority automatically seek the *lowest* place—out of self-preservation if nothing else! To engage in the awesome responsibility of speaking in the name of the Lord, we must be adequately prepared or we may end up doing more damage than good.

If we are wise, we will seek spiritual gifts, but not position or influence. Every bit of influence that we gain from self-promotion or self-seeking will end up being a stumbling block to us. We will end up falling from every platform that we build for ourselves, and the higher we have built it, the farther we will fall. No one can stand the pressures of true spiritual authority who is not standing on a platform that *God* has built. The higher the platform we are standing on, the more everything is magnified—the power and the pressures, the fruit and the damage.

It is not wrong to desire a higher platform if we are desiring it for the right reasons: to glorify the name of the Lord and to accomplish His will. But it *is* wrong for us to build the platform ourselves. As the writer of Hebrews stated concerning the priestly ministry, which is the essence of all ministry: **"And no one takes the honor to himself, but receives it when he is called by God, even as Aaron was. So also Christ did not glorify Himself so as to become a high priest" (Hebrews 5:4-5).** If this is true of the Lord, how much more should it be true of us?

The tares may seem to be everywhere: in the wheat field, in the church, in the prophetic ministry, and in us as individuals. But even though the Lord commands us to let the wheat and tares grow up together, there must be a separation of the tares from the wheat before bread can be made from it. This is often a very uncomfortable process, and can only be done at the right time. It was even said of Jesus that, **"Although He was a Son, He learned obedience from the things which He suffered" (Hebrews 5:8).** How much more should we be willing to suffer the trials and tribulations that will bring us to the maturity required for true spiritual authority?

FOUR

Friends Of God

The Lord has entrusted Himself to the prophets to the degree that He will do *"nothing* **unless He reveals His** *secret* **counsel to His servants the prophets"** **(Amos 3:7).** He has obligated Himself to share everything with His prophets simply because He *wants to*—because the prophets are *His friends.* The foremost calling of a prophet is to be God's friend, someone with whom He can share His most intimate purposes. Only friends and true lovers share their deepest secrets, because they alone can be trusted with them.

The Lord also said that **"the** *secret* **of the LORD is for those who** *fear* **Him"** **(Psalm 25:14).** No king would put up with gossips or those prone to spread the things they heard near his throne, and neither does the Lord. If there is to be a true prophetic voice restored to the church, it must be preceded by a pure, holy and righteous fear of the Lord. Respect for who He is and the preciousness of His word is necessary if there is to be a prophetic ministry with the integrity that such a responsibility requires.

The Fear of God

Elijah's first public statement, given before King Ahab of Israel, was indicative of the first principle of prophetic integrity: **"As the LORD, the God of Israel lives, *before whom I stand...*" (I Kings 17:1).** Elijah was testifying that he was not only standing before Ahab, who was merely a human king; rather, he was standing before the Lord, the King of the universe. Elijah lived his life before the living God, not before men.

The apostle Paul said, **"If I were still trying to please men, I would not be a bond-servant of Christ" (Galatians 1:10).** The degree to which we are seeking the recognition and approval of men is the degree our ministry and word will be corrupted, regardless of how often or how solemnly we attach the addendum, "Thus saith the Lord."

Peter was called "Satan" by Jesus because he tried to counsel Him from the perspective of man's interests rather than God's (see Matthew 16:21-23). We cannot speak a pure word from the Lord until we are delivered from the fear of man and the desire for man's recognition and acceptance. We need to be set free from a perspective that only sees things on the basis of man's interests. When man-centered traits have influence in our lives, we will be prophesying from man's perspective and, like Peter, we will become stumbling blocks to the purposes of God.

Often when we pray for the Lord to bring revival or repentance to an area, He sends a drought to get the people's attention—and we fill the churches to pray for *rain!* Elijah prayed for the Lord's judgments to come because he was of one mind with God, not the people. He also understood that being of one mind with the Lord is ultimately in the best interests of the people. Even God's judgments are in the best interest of the people; if we get them, it is because we need them.

Because of Elijah's uncompromising devotion to God's interests, even when they were in conflict with the desires and lifestyle of the entire nation, he was called the **"troubler of Israel" (I Kings 18:17).** The person who fears God more than man will always be perceived as a threat to man and his interests. The true prophet will in fact be the greatest threat to people's perverted interests, but can also bring great hope for their salvation. It is for this reason that prophets who are overly concerned about what people think of them will never fully walk in their calling, and can easily be changed into false prophets.

A true prophet is the spokesman of God, not the spokesman of the church. Prophets are given for the equipping of the church, not to speak for her. Those who only receive prophets who verify their doctrines, their ministry, or their vision are probably not receiving true prophets. Self-appointed or self-seeking leaders, who are so insecure that they only receive those who agree with them, will always be in conflict with true prophetic ministry and will often be open to false prophetic ministry. And the prophets who only speak what they think will be received by such leaders have perverted the prophetic ministry.

King David is one of the great biblical examples of leadership that has been appointed and established by God. It is said that even Jesus sits upon the throne of David (Luke 1:32). A throne is a seat of authority, and David established a position of authority that even the Lord Jesus could sit upon! Nevertheless, David would not even stop the lunatic who cast stones at him, because he thought God may have sent him to do it (see II Samuel 16:5-13). David did not want to refuse God's rebuke if it was due. That is the nature of true authority, which can only come from a true commissioning by God. David was not concerned about what his people thought of this humiliation; he was more intent on trying to receive what God might be trying to say to him.

David knew that if this lunatic was not sent by God, He would judge him. It was this kind of heart that established David's throne for all generations. In the same way, it is having this heart that will establish our authority and enable it to endure. Those who seek to save their lives, or their positions of authority, will lose them. But those who are willing to lose everything into the hands of God will truly find their lives and be able to keep the authority and positions to which they were appointed. This utter devotion to God's glory and purposes will be required not only from all who desire to walk in the true prophetic anointing, but also from churches that will receive the benefit of that ministry.

A Member of the Body

God gives prophets to speak to the church on His behalf. Although *every* ministry in a sense speaks for the Lord, a prophetic word speaks to a specific situation with a specific revelation of the will and purpose of God concerning it. However, the prophet is just one part of the body of Christ and must function in harmony with the rest of the body.

The prophet is like the nervous system which carries signals from the brain to the rest of the body. Although its primary function is to represent the head and connect it to the rest of the body, the nervous system also carries some signals (such as pain) from the body back to the brain. The prophet, likewise, must stand in the place of both messenger and intercessor.

The Lord has by no means limited Himself to speaking only through those called as prophets, but that is the primary function of a prophet. Similarly, even though the Lord may choose to use *anyone* for healing the sick, whether the person has a special gift of healing or not, the one who has this gift will be especially devoted to it. As the apostle Paul explained, everyone is not a foot or an eye, for **"if the whole body were an eye, where would the hearing be?" (I Corinthians 12:17).**

Paul also said, **"You can *all* prophesy one by one" (I Corinthians 14:31).** Even though the foot is not the eye, when it is dark and one cannot use his eyes, he may stick out his foot to "see" where he is going. While the Lord does appoint many believers to *specialize* in a ministry, that does not mean those are the only ones He will ever use for that ministry. Not everyone is a prophet, but all may prophesy.

Every member of the body is different. We cannot expect other ministers to be like prophets, nor the prophets to be like other ministers. Actually, every prophet in Scripture was different from all of the other prophets. It is the nature of the Lord to be creative. He makes every person, every tree, and even every snowflake different. When we limit the Lord, or the things of the Lord, to a certain pattern or formula, we have greatly limited our ability to relate to Him and hear from Him.

Some prophets in the Bible received revelation primarily through visions, others through dreams, others by the word of the Lord, others by discerning His purposes in current events, others through the Scriptures, and others in trances. Some were caught up into the heavenlies so that they were not just seeing a vision—they were *there*. Others received revelation from angels, others directly from the Lord. He may speak to us one way now, and the next time speak to us in an entirely different manner. He does not do this to confuse us, but to keep us seeking Him and dependent on Him.

"The testimony of Jesus is the spirit of prophecy" (Revelation 19:10). All true prophecy is His testimony. It comes from Him and draws us to Him. It is what He is saying to His church. Jesus has manifested Himself in different ways—He is a lion and He is also a lamb. He came as the Prince of Peace, and yet He said He came to bring a sword. These aspects of His nature do not contradict; they compliment each other and give us a more complete revelation of Him.

This is why the apostle entreated the Romans to **"behold then the kindness *and* severity of God" (Romans 11:22).** We must behold both His kindness and His severity if we are to have an accurate revelation of His nature. Those who only see His kindness, mercy and forgiveness have almost inevitably fallen into the bondage of presumptuous grace and unsanctified mercy. Unsanctified mercy is having mercy for things of which God disapproves. Those who only see His severity often become "sheep beaters" who minister more in the spirit of **"the accuser of our brethren" (Revelation 12:10)** than in the Spirit of Jesus, who ever lives to intercede for us (Hebrews 7:25).

Prophets of Christ

We must not be "prophets of grace" or "prophets of judgment," but rather prophets who give the testimony of *Jesus*. Different countries, and even different parts of countries, are under different controlling spirits, or principalities. For each country or region, the Lord has a specific message—truth prescribed to set people free from these controlling spirits of darkness.

For example, the southern United States is generally under a religious spirit that promulgates doctrines and mind-sets that lead to self-righteousness. In the Midwest there tends to be almost the opposite problem. There you will find a critical spirit that has driven the people to a sense of unworthiness and an inability to believe that God really loves and accepts them. However, much of the preaching in the South is an overemphasis on God's kindness, and this has promoted a false concept of grace and a false view of prosperity. Generally, the South needs to hear more about the severity of God, while the Midwest needs to hear more about His kindness.

Those who preach or prophesy must be sensitive to what Jesus is saying in the place where they are, and must not just come with a general message of kindness or severity. If we carry the general message of severity to those who are already beaten down by the accuser, we will be feeding that condemning spirit instead of the Spirit and testimony of Jesus. The same is true if we are prone to only preach His kindness. The true prophet will not be "locked in" to a message of mercy, judgment or any other position, but will speak the present mind of Christ for each situation.

When John received the Revelation, each of the seven churches in Asia Minor needed a different message, even though they existed in the same region at the same period of time. This shows that when we try to give a single message to the whole church, we will seldom really have the mind of the Lord. John received these messages for the churches by being caught up in the Spirit and receiving them from the Lord, not by going to the churches and trying to judge their condition or needs. Pastors and teachers can sometimes discern the needs for shepherding and teaching by just being with a church and observing it, but that is not how prophets operate. To give the appropriate *prophetic* message to a church, we must see the Lord, not the people.

Jesus is the Lion *and* the Lamb. Sometimes He speaks in a **"still small voice" (I Kings 19:12 KJV),** and at other times He **"roars from Zion" (Joel 3:16).** If we can only hear the still small voice, we will miss Him when He roars, and vice versa. It is not *how* God speaks that enables us to recognize Him—it is the *Spirit* that is speaking that we must discern. I know my wife's voice whether she whispers or raises her voice, because I know *her.* If we know the Lord, we will recognize His voice regardless of the manner in which He speaks.

Growing in the Prophetic

One of the most common questions asked of me is, "How does one grow in the prophetic ministry?" Although this is not really an improper question, until it is changed somewhat we may never mature in a true ministry of any type. We are not called primarily to grow up into a *ministry;* **"we are to grow up in all aspects *into Him"* (Ephesians 4:15).** An apple tree does not have to strive to produce apples; apples will grow because of the kind of tree it is. To walk in true ministry, we must be delivered from a fallacy of the Industrial Age— the need to have a formula for everything. The real issue of ministry is not *how* we do it, but *Whom* we are abiding in while we do it.

There is no formula or "how to" for becoming prophetic. If God has not called us as a prophet, it cannot be generated by self-effort. We can ask for spiritual gifts and receive them, but the existence of gifts in our lives doesn't necessarily mean we have an office of ministry in the church. If the Lord has called us to a certain ministry, it will be evident in the right season.

It is not wrong to desire a ministry, as long as we desire it for the right reason—which is to serve the purpose of God. When that is our motive, we are able to maintain the simplicity of devotion to Christ. Ministry, then, is but a means for serving Him. When ministry itself is our emphasis, it will be a tainted ministry at best. If testifying *of Him* is our central devotion, we are close to that which is truly prophetic, which is **"the testimony of Jesus."** As the Lord warned, **"He who speaks from himself seeks his own glory [or recognition]; but He who is seeking the glory [or recognition] of the one who sent Him, He is true" (John 7:18).**

Regardless of which ministry we are called to, we must not copy or emulate other people, but rather the One whose image we are called to bear. Schools for prophets may be helpful, but they will be counterproductive if they just bring forth "parrots" who all prophesy the same things. Sadly, I can tell the denomination of most ministers by their clothes and, in some cases, by the cars they drive. Where does this compulsion toward uniformity come from? It is contrary to both the natural creation and the new creation.

There is a place for learning from those who are our elders and who have gone before us, and there is a true discipleship that must be restored to the church. However, true discipleship must allow the unique gifts and calling of each individual to come forth. It must prepare people and point them to an increasingly direct relationship with the Lord. Even though we may love and appreciate our natural parents, and may occasionally turn to them for counsel even when we are grown, there is a time when we must become the heads of our own families. Wise parents prepare their children for that time, which means helping them to become increasingly independent.

Not Forsaking the Assembling

One must first learn to be independent before it will be possible to attain the highest form of maturity—*inter*dependence. Healthy relationships are based on interdependence, not co-dependence. Before we can achieve this, we must come to know and be secure in our own identity. It would be hard for a hand to properly function with the rest of the body if it did not know that it was a hand, or did not know the proper functions of a hand. Without this knowledge, it might one day try to be a foot, the next day an ear, etc. Is this not what we see so often in the church?

The biblical exhortation to **"not [forsake] the assembling of ourselves together" (Hebrews 10:25 KJV)** was not just referring to church meetings, but also to the way in which the different parts must be assembled together to make a whole. The real school and crucible of the prophetic ministry comes as we properly learn to fit and function with the rest of the body of Christ. This is because Jesus was not just a prophet; He was THE Shepherd, THE Evangelist, THE Teacher, and THE Apostle. His prophetic ministry flowed in perfect harmony with the other aspects of His ministry. All who walk in true prophetic ministry will fit with the other ministries as well.

Unlike their Old Testament counterparts, New Testament prophets are a part of a body of different ministries which must all function together in order to be complete. In Christ no ministry is to be independent of the others, but all are interdependent and must work as one unit. A prophet's ultimate identity cannot be realized without being properly joined to the Head and to the rest of His body.

Neither will any of the other ministries be complete without the prophet. Paul said that "we" have the mind of Christ, not "I" (see I Corinthians 2:16). It is as we all come together that we have His mind and His ministry. When Jesus ascended on high and gave "gifts" to men (Ephesians 4:8), He was giving *Himself* to men.

As stated, Jesus is THE Apostle, Prophet, Evangelist, Pastor and Teacher. Now that these aspects of His ministry are given to individuals, all of these gifted individuals must come together in order to have the complete ministry of Christ. This is why Paul also explained to the Corinthians that **"the testimony concerning Christ was confirmed in you, so that you are *not lacking in any gift"* (I Corinthians 1:6-7).** The complete testimony of Christ can only be presented by all of the gifts and ministries functioning together as one unit. Jesus prayed for His people to be *"perfected* [literally, made complete] *in unity"* (John 17:23).

The writer of Hebrews opened his epistle, **"God, after He spoke long ago to the fathers in the prophets in many portions and in many ways, in these last days has spoken to us IN HIS SON" (Hebrews 1:1-2).** The Old Covenant prophets were prophesying *of* Jesus who was to come; the New Covenant prophets are prophesying *in* Jesus, as members of His very body. New Covenant prophesying is to be in harmony with the full revelation of His Person, nature and commission, as manifested in the rest of the gifts and ministries distributed to the church.

Why We Must Emphasize the Prophetic

We have come to a period in which the prophetic ministry will be emphasized, and, for a time, it needs to be.

It must be fully restored as a vital part of the ministry of Christ in His church. If it is restored properly, it will bring about a greater realization and more complete restoration of the other ministries as well. They are *all* required for the complete testimony of Christ, and for the complete fulfillment of their own purpose and function.

No ministry which rejects or avoids what is now happening in the restoration of the prophetic ministry will be able to truly fulfill its own calling and purpose in this hour. Prophets who reject or avoid integration into the rest of the body of Christ are not true New Covenant prophets, regardless of their gifts or the accuracy of their doctrine. Today the Father is speaking *"in His Son"* **(Hebrews 1:2).** It is true that one can be "joined to the church," according to the popular interpretations of what that means, without genuinely being joined to the Head. But no one can be properly joined to the Head without also being joined to His body, the church.

PART II

FIVE

Why We Need Prophets Today

Why do we need prophets today? Do we not have the Scriptures that contain the whole counsel of God? Yes, the Bible *is* the complete, sufficient, inerrant Word of God, and is the only foundation upon which we base Christian doctrine. But it was never intended to be the *whole* counsel of God. If it were, we would not need the Holy Spirit.

If we say that the Scriptures make spiritual gifts and prophetic ministries obsolete, we would have to also conclude that none of the other ministries are still necessary either. This is obviously not the case. The biblical ministries such as pastors, teachers and prophets have a different function than the written Word, as do spiritual gifts. All are needed if we are to be thoroughly equipped. The gifts of the Holy Spirit do not replace the Bible, but neither does the Bible replace the gifts of the Holy Spirit.

The relationship between the written Word and the gift of prophecy is the same as it has always been. After repeating the entire Law to the nation of Israel, Moses gave a remarkable exhortation:

> **Now it shall come to pass, if you diligently obey the *voice* of the LORD your God, to observe carefully all His commandments which I command you today, that the LORD your God will set you high above all nations of the earth (Deuteronomy 28:1 NKJV).**

So under the Law, when seemingly every detail of the people's relationships to the Lord and to one another had been mandated, they were nevertheless exhorted to obey the *voice* of the Lord. The proper relationship of Israel to the Lord required that they obey *both* His written Word and His voice.

Even with all the exhaustive commandments of the Law of Moses, the written Word did not cover every aspect of life or every major decision that would have to be made by God's people. For example, there was nothing in the written Word that gave Joshua the instructions for taking Jericho. Joshua and the other leaders of Israel had to receive specific instructions from the Lord that simply were not covered in the written Word.

Likewise, Joshua's mistake in relation to the Gibeonites did not happen just because he did not know the Law, but because he did not seek a special revelation of the Lord's counsel in the matter (see Joshua 9). Such matters were not covered in the Law—Joshua needed to hear directly from the Lord. This same principle was clearly demonstrated in the example of the first-century church, and is still a vital need of the church today.

What if the written Word *did* cover every aspect of life? Then it would not only be impractical because of its size, but there would be no place for developing a personal relationship with the Lord Himself, which is the essence of true Christianity.

In John 16:7, Jesus told His disciples, **"It is to your advantage that I go away; for if I do not go away, the Helper shall not come to you; but if I go, I will send Him to you."** The Lord did not say that it was to their advantage that He was going away because He was going to give them a book! The Lord also said that His sheep know His *voice* (see John 10:4); He did not say that His sheep know His *book*. It is the Holy Spirit who convicts the world of sin, reveals Jesus, and leads us into all truth.

Without the Holy Spirit, **"the letter kills" (II Corinthians 3:6).** But with the Holy Spirit, the Bible is one of the most powerful tools that we have been given. It is essential for maintaining sound doctrine. In Matthew 22:29 (NIV) Jesus said, **"You are in error because you do not know the Scriptures or the power of God."** We will fall into error if we do not know *both* God's written Word and His power. We have been given both because we need both.

Jesus is the Word of God personified, and those who love Him cannot help but love the written Word and esteem it as the priceless treasure that it is. We must be able to hear the Lord's voice when He speaks, but we must not go to the extreme of expecting to hear His voice for everything. Much of the counsel He expects us to get is already contained in His written Word.

Until We Reach Full Stature

Paul wrote to the Ephesians:

He [Jesus] gave some as apostles, and some as prophets and some as evangelists and some as pastors and teachers,

for the equipping of the saints for the work of service, to the building up of the body of Christ;

***UNTIL* we all attain to the unity of the faith, and of the knowledge of the Son of God, to a mature man, to the measure of the stature which belongs to the fulness of Christ (Ephesians 4:11-13).**

That the Lord has given prophets to His church as an integral part of her ministry can hardly be questioned if we believe the Bible. However, the question for many is not if prophets were given as a part of the *original* ministry of the church, but whether they are a part of the church's *present* ministry.

The prophetic ministry, along with the other ministries mentioned in this text, were given *"until"* the church matures to **"the measure of the stature which belongs to the fulness of Christ."** For us to say that this ministry no longer exists is also to say that the church has come to complete maturity and a stature corresponding to the fulness of Christ. This is one argument that no one seems ready to make, so we can conclude that the prophetic ministry is still required if we are going to attain the level of maturity God intends for us.

We can therefore boldly state, based on the Scriptures, that a rejection of the gifts and ministries the Lord ordained for the equipping of His church is a fundamental cause of the church's immaturity and confusion. We must receive a prophet *in the name of a prophet* if we are to receive a **"prophet's reward,"** or the benefit of prophetic ministry (Matthew 10:41). If we receive a prophet as just a teacher, that is all we are going to get—teaching. If we receive a prophet in the name of a prophet, we will get the reward of the prophetic ministry, which we must clearly have if we are going to grow up in all aspects into Christ.

This principle applies to all the other gifts and ministries given to the church as well. If we do not receive pastors with the true authority of their position, but rather see them as mere administrators, we will not receive a pastor's reward. If we receive an apostle as just a teacher, all we will get is teaching instead of the full benefit of the apostolic ministry.

Jesus Is THE Prophet

Receiving any ministry in the name of that ministry is essential if we are to receive the fulness of Christ into our midst. Each of these ministries are vessels for the Lord Jesus to manifest Himself to His church and equip her for the service to which she has been called. We should not recognize people as teachers just because they have the ability to expound the Scriptures eloquently and accurately, but only when we see our Teacher, Jesus, in them. We should not receive people as pastors just because they have seminary degrees or even because of their ability to lead and care for people; we should only recognize those as pastors in whom we see our Shepherd.

When the Lord lamented over Jerusalem, He declared, **"From now on you shall not see ME until you say, 'Blessed is He who comes in the name of the Lord!'" (Matthew 23:39)** If we cannot see Him in those whom He sends, we will not see Him at all. If the Lord sends us a teacher whom we reject, we are rejecting the Teacher Himself. If we reject a prophet He has sent to us, we are rejecting the Lord's own prophetic ministry. But if we receive those whom He sends, we are receiving Him.

Jesus said, **"Truly I say to you, to the extent that you did it to one of these brothers of Mine, even the least of them, you did it to *Me*" (Matthew 25:40).** When we reject any one of the ministries the Lord has established, we are rejecting that whole aspect of *Him*. The real question is not whether or not there are prophets today, but rather whether we are open to receiving from them.

The great test before the Laodicean church was to hear the Lord knocking. Since Laodicea was the last of the churches which the Lord addressed, it is a prophecy to the last-day church in particular. The greatest test of the church today is to hear the Lord knocking so that we can open to let Him in. It is noteworthy that He said, **"Behold, I stand at the door and knock; *if anyone hears My voice and opens...*"** **(Revelation 3:20).** Many are hearing His knock, but only those who hear His *voice* will open to Him.

When he puts forth all his own, he goes before them, *and the sheep follow him because they know his voice.*

And a stranger they simply will not follow, but will flee from him, because they do not know the voice of strangers (John 10:4-5).

The essence of the prophetic ministry is to know the voice of the Lord and to equip the church to know His voice, so that His sheep can follow Him.

He Still Comes in a "Different Form"

After Jesus' resurrection, even His closest disciples had trouble recognizing Him, because **"He appeared in a different form" (Mark 16:12).** This was done purposely, so that His disciples could no longer depend on His physical appearance to recognize Him. How often do we miss Him too when He tries to draw close to us, because He comes **"in a different form"?** If we are to receive Jesus, we cannot be dependent on "forms" for recognizing Him; we must know Him after the Spirit, not externals. We must know His voice.

One of the chief issues for the last-day church is to hear Him knocking and hear His voice. He is coming to us again with apostles and prophets, but we must understand that they will all be different. Every prophet in Scripture is different from the other ones. All of the apostles were very different from each other, and their ministries were also different.

Just as the Lord makes every snowflake different, He obviously delights in diversity. His whole creation reflects the fact that the Creator is ultimate Creativity. Since this is so obviously true, why is the church so boringly uniform? There have been very few institutions which have stifled creativity more than the institution of the church. This reflects just how radical our departure has been from the true Spirit and nature of the Lord.

In Scripture, water is often symbolic of the word (see Ephesians 5:26). Metaphors are used in Scripture because the characteristics they have are consistent with the characteristics of that which they portray. Like water, the living word must continue to *flow* if it is to stay pure. For that reason, the Lord continues to come to us in different "forms." If we are recognizing Him after the Spirit and not just the form, He will continually be fresh to us. Adopting this perspective will deliver us from the tragic historical compulsion of spiritual movements to settle into a certain form and then stop flowing.

Jesus is coming back for a bride **"having no spot or wrinkle" (Ephesians 5:27).** That she is without spot speaks of her purity; that she is without wrinkle speaks of her ability to stay youthful. She is able to do this because the Lord keeps the relationship fresh and exciting—He is new every morning.

When the Lord comes to us in a different form than we are used to, it works to keep us fresh in spirit. This combats our tendency to become rigid and inflexible, the nature of wineskins which can no longer receive new wine (see Luke 5:37-39). Because prophets often seem to be cast from a different mold than the rest of the church, they are able to serve as a primary vehicle to help the church maintain this openness to the Spirit.

The natural man cannot receive the things of the Spirit (see I Corinthians 2:14). As one of my friends says, "The Lord often offends the minds so that He can reveal the hearts." Saul of Tarsus is one of the great biblical examples of a religious man who tried to live by his natural mind. Saul had to be struck blind in the natural so that he could see in the Spirit. Though this may not happen to us as quickly and dramatically as it did to the great apostle, it is a process that we must all go through.

The Ultimate Goal of Prophetic Ministry

The Lord's ultimate goal through the New Testament prophetic ministry is not just to give the church prophecies, but to bring the church to the place where we **"can *all* prophesy" (I Corinthians 14:31).** The prophets, like the other equipping gift ministries, are not given just to perform their own ministry, but for **"the equipping of the saints for the work of service" (Ephesians 4:12).**

The New Testament prophet's primary function is to open the church to the ministry of Jesus *the* Prophet so that He can flow freely among His people. Everyone is not called to the office of a prophet, but the whole church, as a unit, is called to be a prophet to the world, manifesting Christ's ministry as the Spokesman for God.

When Israel was told to partake of the Passover, they were told that they had to eat the entire lamb and **"not leave any of it" (Exodus 12:9-10).** We must receive *all* of Jesus if we are to receive Him at all. As Paul instructed the Corinthians, **"the testimony concerning Christ was confirmed in you** *so that you are not lacking in ANY gift"* **(I Corinthians 1:6-7).** The true testimony of Christ is confirmed in the church when He is able to freely move in any way that He chooses. This is profound evidence that He has found a place to lay His head— a place where He *is* the Head.

We must understand that ministries seldom come in the packages that we would expect. The Lord chooses the foolish things of the world to confound the wise (I Corinthians 1:27). He chose Paul, the Pharisee of Pharisees, to be the apostle of grace. He chose Peter, the most unstable of the twelve, to be "Petra," the rock. If we allow His grace to work, He will make some of the most unlikely people into mighty apostles and prophets. Likewise, some of the vessels who appear most promising in our eyes will prove to be false.

Open the Door to Only Him

One of the ultimate tests of the last-day church will be to hear the Lord's knock and His voice, and then open the doors of our hearts to Him. However, this will require us to also recognize when a knock or a voice is not His. It is foolish to allow entrance to everyone who claims to be a prophet. Neither can those who have responsibility for the flock of God allow it to become a target for potshots from prophets in training.

There is not an infallible person alive, and words from even the most mature prophets must be judged (I Corinthians 14:29). It is not quenching the Spirit to properly judge prophecies and the prophets who give them (see I Thessalonians 5:20-21).

Much more will be said about false prophets and false prophecy in a later chapter. Here we are concerned about establishing orderly and safe ways for prophets and other ministries to mature in our congregations without constant confusion and injury to the people. Once we understand that this is an essential part of the ministry the Lord has given to His church, we must seek to understand how it is supposed to fit with the other equipping ministries He has established. There must be the freedom for diversity to be expressed, but in God's diversity there is also harmony.

The Lord said, **"The harvest is the end of the age" (Matthew 13:39).** This harvest is the reaping of everything that has been sown, both good and evil. **"Many false prophets will arise and will mislead many" (Matthew 24:11).** This is another warning that there will be tares mixed in with the wheat. The tares are maturing right along with the wheat. Our greatest protection from the false is to know what is real. If we do not know that which is real, we will become increasingly subject to the false.

If one does not plant anything in a field, will wheat just grow on its own? Of course not; that field will be overcome with weeds and tares. The same is true of the church. If we allow the Lord to plant the wheat of the prophetic ministry, there will be some tares mixed in. Even so, if we do not allow Him to plant the wheat, we will have nothing but the tares.

To face the times properly, we must be delivered from our knee-jerk reaction to problems and realize that the Lord allows all of them for our maturity. The greatest Leader of all, Jesus, chose Judas and placed him right in His top level of leadership—even though He knew what a scoundrel Judas was! Who are we to think that we have a better way than the Lord?

Gaining Discernment

Learning to deal with the tares is a part of the curriculum of the kingdom. Every time we must deal with a false prophet or a betrayer, our true discernment will grow dramatically. We must not waste these valuable trials by deciding not to play the game anymore, but rather we must let them make us even more resolute in our determination to find that which is true. Our ultimate victory is assured, if we do not quit.

Many people, churches and movements have entirely rejected the prophetic because they were wounded by false prophets or the mistakes of the immature. And many who have been called to prophetic ministry have rejected this call because of their own mistakes. However, the Scriptures clearly show that God almost never raises up a great leader who does not make serious mistakes. Some of the greatest leaders made some of the greatest mistakes, but they did not let that stop them.

If we do not give up, we will ultimately succeed. Those who allow their own mistakes to stop them are walking by faith not in God, but in themselves. Our mistakes will, and should, erode the confidence that we have in ourselves, but we must not allow them to erode our faith in God.

True faith in God does not put confidence in the flesh (Philippians 3:3). That is why God did not call Abraham, the "father of faith," until he was seemingly too old to accomplish his destiny—and then made him wait many more years before the fulfillment came. If we are going to have the true promised seed of God, we must be willing to be brought to the place where we know that it is impossible for us to do it. That is the essence of true faith—total dependency on God.

As we proceed in this study, we will examine the false and the true. We will look at the stumbling blocks and the stepping stones. It is important that we be able to recognize both. We must also realize that many of the things that have been stumbling blocks to us, such as our own mistakes, were meant to be stepping stones.

Over the years I have noticed that some of those who have made the greatest advances in prophetic ministry and gifts were the very ones who had previously made some of the most embarrassing mistakes. Their advances usually came right after a great mistake. In fact, their one common denominator was that they did not let the mistakes stop them. Humbling themselves by acknowledging the mistakes, they kept on going, trusting a little less in themselves, but determined to trust even more in the Lord.

Is that not one of the great lessons of the Song of Solomon? When the love journey was over, the bride came up out of the wilderness **"leaning on her beloved" (Song of Solomon 8:5).** When our journey is over, that will also be our posture with Him. It is for His sake that we must not quit.

SIX

The Source Of True Spiritual Authority

In previous chapters we established why it is important for the church to receive the prophetic ministry. In this chapter we will address why it is important for prophets to properly relate to the church. We will also consider some common mistakes made by those called to walk in this difficult ministry.

Conflict and Rejection

The prophetic ministry has a built-in factor that causes misunderstanding and rejection. This factor is the supernatural, and often bizarre, experiences which are common with this calling. To effectively walk in the prophetic ministry, one has to become comfortable with uncommon and extraordinary experiences. These may include angelic visitations, trances, being transported geographically in the Spirit, being caught up into heavenly places, etc.

All of these experiences are biblically established as "normal" for the prophetic. Even so, such experiences are very hard to understand for those who have not had them. This often leads to doubt and rejection of the emerging prophet.

There is a legitimate fear caused by the emergence of New Age and other cults who tout similar experiences, but which are demonic. However, as already stated, there would be no counterfeit money if there were not real money. There would be no counterfeit prophetic experiences if there were not also true ones.

One reason there is such an increase of demonic activity in the area of supernatural experiences is to confuse the church so that she will reject the real gifts and experiences which the Lord is restoring to her. Satan knows that these are essential to the accomplishing of God's purposes in this last hour, and he can be expected to do all he can to muddy these waters. The best way for us to help clear up the mess he is making is to find the pure source of the stream.

We have come to the time of the great power conflict of the ages. The power of the cults and the New Age Movement is increasing dramatically, but the Lord has not left His people without power to face this evil onslaught. "**When the enemy shall come in like a flood, the spirit of the LORD shall lift up a standard against him**" (Isaiah 59:19 KJV). As the power of cults has been increasing, the power given to the church has been increasing even more. Cults have begun receiving supernatural revelation about Christian leaders in order to begin systematic attacks on them. However, the Lord has begun raising up prophets to discern the enemy's schemes so that the church can start ambushing him, turning his evil strategy into his own trap.

As we proceed toward the conclusion of this age, the conflict between light and darkness will become increasingly supernatural. The day when it was possible to take a neutral stance toward the supernatural is over. If we do not know the true power of God's Spirit, we will become increasingly subject to the power of the evil one. Those whose fears or doctrines have led them to avoid even the Lord's supernatural power will soon find themselves and their children easy prey for evil supernatural powers.

Mankind was created to have fellowship with God, Who is Spirit. Those who worship Him can *only* worship Him in spirit and truth. Because we were created to have spiritual fellowship and worship, a void exists which draws us to the spiritual and the supernatural. If this is not fulfilled by the Spirit of Truth, who leads us to worship the Lord in spirit and truth, we will be deceived by the spirit of error. As C.S. Lewis observed, "If you deny a man food, he will gobble poison." If we deny people access to a proper supernatural relationship with God, they will succumb to the oppression and seductions of evil supernatural power.

Few things will test the degree of our Christlikeness more than rejection. God allows rejection in our lives to help reveal and deliver us from our own evil motives. If we feel rejected when people ostracize us, it only reveals that we are not yet dead to this world. It is impossible for a dead man to feel rejection! Jesus, knowing that on the very next day His best friends were going to betray Him, deny Him, and flee from Him in His hour of need, earnestly desired to have one last meal with them! And then He even went out of His way to express His love for them and wash their feet! How many of us would be this selfless?

Rejection is an inevitable companion of true ministry, and it provides one of our greatest opportunities to operate in Jesus' love. To be able to handle rejection without being offended is one of the great demonstrations of spiritual maturity, which is Christlikeness.

Motivated by Love

Mature prophets can discern spirits; immature prophets are often fooled by them. Many who were called as true prophets of God have been seduced by the enemy because they refused the protection and covering of the rest of the body of Christ. Often this refusal to properly relate to the church stems from painful experiences in which the prophet was misunderstood or rejected by church leaders in the past. The Lord allows such misunderstandings because learning to deal correctly with rejection and authority is essential for anyone who is going to carry the awesome power and responsibility of having supernatural revelation.

Discernment of spirits is a primary gift through which the prophetic ministry must function. It is fundamental that we first discern the source of spiritual revelation. But much of what is called "discernment" today is really nothing more than suspicion. This often has its root more in self-preservation or retaliation than in the love of Christ. True spiritual discernment is rooted in love, which Paul describes in I Corinthians 13:4-7:

> **Love is patient, love is kind, and is not jealous; love does not brag and is not arrogant,**
>
> **does not act unbecomingly; it does not seek its own, is not provoked, does not take into account a wrong suffered,**
>
> **does not rejoice in unrighteousness, but rejoices with the truth;**
>
> **bears all things, believes all things, hopes all things, endures all things.**

Any motivation other than love will distort our discernment. This is why Paul prayed for the Philippians' *love* to **"abound**

still more and more *in real knowledge and all discernment"*
(Philippians 1:9). Love and true discernment cannot
be separated.

God is love (I John 4:8), and if we are going to speak for
Him, we must also abide in His love. Sometimes His love is
severe and brings discipline, but it is love nevertheless. Even
God's judgment is a manifestation of His love. We only have
true spiritual authority over areas for which He has given us
His love. Only when we are ministering from a foundation
of His love will our discernment be true.

As Romans 11:29 states, **"The gifts and the calling of
God are irrevocable."** The Lord is faithful even when we
are unfaithful. When the Lord gives a gift He will not take
it back, even if we become unfaithful or misuse it. This is
why those who have valid gifts of healing or miracles can
fall into sin or corruption, but the gifts will still operate. The
same is true of the gifts of prophecy, a word of wisdom, or
a word of knowledge.

When God gives a gift, He does not take it back if we fall.
This is why it is so important that we judge a ministry by the
fruit rather than by impressive gifts of the Spirit. Those who
move in the power and revelatory gifts, yet who are affected
by rejection or rebellion, can use the gifts of God to bring
division and damage to the very work of God. This is a

dynamic which may be hard to understand, but it stems from the faithfulness of the Lord.

Unhealed Spiritual Wounds

Under the Old Covenant, priests were not allowed to minister if they had scabs, which are unhealed wounds (see Leviticus 21:20). When one had scabs, others could not touch them. The same is true of us; when we have unhealed spiritual wounds, others cannot get close to us and we cannot function in our true priestly ministry. Most of us have witnessed those who preach, prophesy or minister out of their own rejection, bitterness or other unhealed wounds—it is a corruption of their ministry.

As Paul explained to Timothy, **"The goal of our instruction is *love* from a pure heart and a good conscience and a sincere faith" (I Timothy 1:5).** Paul also exhorted the Corinthians to **"desire earnestly spiritual gifts" (I Corinthians 14:1),** but he never exhorted them to make gifts their goal. We need the gifts and the power of the Spirit. In fact, we need *much more* power than we are presently walking in. But we need them for the sake of ministering to hurting people, not just to establish our own ministries or to have big conferences. When we lose sight of the goal—which is love from a pure heart, a good conscience, and a sincere faith—we have lost our way.

All of the gifts of the Spirit operate by faith, and faith works through love (see Galatians 5:6). True faith is not just the confidence that God *can* do certain things, it is knowing that He *wants* to do them, because He loves us. Although fear is the opposite of faith, it is conquered when we are filled with the love of God: **"There is no fear in love; but perfect love casts out fear" (I John 4:18).** Love casts out everything that hinders the move of God through us and to us. Love is the foundation upon which spiritual authority and the gifts of the Spirit operate. It is vain to seek the gifts until they have this foundation to be built upon. The stronger the foundation, the more power that can be entrusted to us.

Understanding this, some have been fond of saying that they "do not seek the gifts, but the Giver." Not only is this an overreaction, it is also contrary to the scripture that exhorts us to **"Pursue love, yet earnestly desire spiritual gifts" (I Corinthians 14:1).** Paul is saying here that love and desiring spiritual gifts are not mutually exclusive. We should pursue love and the fruit of the Spirit *first*, but that does not mean that we should not pursue the gifts too. We should pursue both. If we have the true love of God, we will **"earnestly desire"** spiritual gifts so that we can do something with our love.

True Maturity

Most who are called to the prophetic ministry endure much rejection and misunderstanding so that they can learn to overcome such things. If we are to accomplish the purposes of God, we must come to the level of maturity where **"the love of Christ controls us" (II Corinthians 5:14).** Love does not take into account the wrongs suffered and is not motivated by rejection, which drives us to retaliation or trying to prove ourselves.

Spiritual gifts which are not motivated by love are **"a noisy gong or a clanging cymbal" (I Corinthians 13:1).** Gifts of the Spirit which are not grounded in love are usually *noisy*. These will come with fanfare and hype that are motivated by self-promotion. A noisy gong or clanging cymbal will also make the Lord's trumpet call harder to hear. But a person who is controlled by the love of Christ will be consumed by the sole desire to see Him glorified.

True love is tolerant and patient. There is certainly a place for calling the church to maturity and to obedience to Christ; indeed, this is a basic part of the calling of the prophet. But it must be done in love and not in impatience or intolerance. We need to occasionally look back at our own spiritual lives just five, 10 or 15 years ago. Are we being impatient with those who are now at the same levels that we were then? In many cases they are probably further along than we were.

Much of the church is immature because it is *supposed to be* immature! A two-year-old child is supposed to be immature. A two-year-old may still need to wear diapers, and that is okay. However, if a 15-year-old is still having to wear them, we have a problem! I do not want my two-year-old to try and do the things a six-year-old can do. That will inevitably frustrate him, and it could also do serious damage to his soul if I expect such maturity from him before he is capable of it.

I want my children to be disciplined and mature for their present age levels, but I must not require more of them than that. We must have the same patience with those in the church. We must be discerning of their present spiritual level, and call them to the proper discipline and maturity commensurate with it.

Ministries that are working for the equipping of the church must be careful not to put their own expectations on the church, but to seek the Lord for His expectations. Ministers who have not been healed of previous rejections often take their next assignment with a determination to prove their competency. This often causes them to put unrealistic pressures on both themselves and those they are ministering to, which only leads to more failures. This can be a vicious cycle, leaving not only a long line of wounded people, but also ministers who are either too bitter or too insecure to function in their callings.

When we know that we have received our commission from above, and that we are known by the Father, it really does not matter what people think of us. This realization brings a liberation that is utterly essential for any minister. We cannot function in true ministry if we are carrying any yoke other than the Lord's. We must not allow ourselves to be controlled by human expectations, or even our own expectations, but only by the Lord's. He does not expect of us what He does not empower us to perform.

Stripes and Healing

Jesus experienced the greatest rejection the world has ever known, or will ever know. He was rejected by the world that He Himself had made. Coming in love, He healed and delivered the oppressed, and He never once committed a sin. Yet, in return for all the good that He had done, He suffered the most cruel and humiliating death—and He suffered it for the very ones who killed Him. He turned the greatest evil and the greatest injustice the world had ever known into the opportunity to forgive and save the very ones who persecuted Him.

The Lord commands those who follow Him to do the same thing: We must take up our crosses every day, just as

He did (Luke 9:23). If we do, we have the power to overcome evil with good. Every evil that is done has a counterbalancing potential to be used for good. When we turn evil into good, it delivers men from the evil that is in them. As ministers of the gospel, we are certain to be rejected—but we can turn each rejection into an opportunity to show the love of God.

It is by the Lord's stripes that we are healed. In the very place where He was wounded, He received authority for healing. The same principle works for us. The Lord does not do the wounding, but He allows the enemy to do it for our sake and the sake of those we are called to serve. If we receive wounds as the blessing that He declares them to be, they become sources of authority for healing others who are wounded.

In this way, one who has been subject to child abuse will have compassion for others who are suffering abuse. Compassion is the foundation of all true spiritual authority. When Jesus felt compassion for the sheep without a shepherd, He became their Shepherd. Many of those with the greatest healing ministries in history have endured painful physical maladies themselves or were touched by the suffering of those close to them.

We must see that every trial that comes our way is for the purpose of causing us to grow in spiritual authority. Every test is for the purpose of promotion. That is why the apostle

Paul defended his own authority by pointing to the beatings, stonings and great trials that he had endured for the sake of the gospel (II Corinthians 11:23-33). *Do not waste your trials!*

Mercy and Judgment

The essence of all that God is doing on the earth is found in redemption. He is turning all that the enemy meant for evil into a great and ultimate good. However, some people reject the love and mercy of the Lord to the degree that they become incorrigible, which means that they are beyond help. This happened to Judas. At this point, God's mercy is replaced with judgment. But we must understand that **"Mercy triumphs over judgment" (James 2:13).**

The Lord's patience with people greatly exceeds what we are usually willing to endure before pronouncing judgment. Just as most parents are more patient with their own children than they are with others, the Lord is usually far more patient with His children than we are. He sent His own Son to be tortured and killed for them because He loves them. If the Son of God could suffer such cruelty and injustice for their sake, how much more should we be willing to suffer for the sake of extending His great salvation?

It is also true that at times we can be far more tolerant of evil than God is. This is what I call "unsanctified mercy." It is showing mercy to those the Lord wants to put under judgment. Either extreme can cause us to misrepresent the

Lord. Therefore we must always remember that we only have true spiritual authority to the degree that the King Himself abides within us, and we abide in Him. He is the One to whom all rule, authority and power has been given. To walk in true spiritual authority is simply to abide in Him, to be sensitive to His leading, and to be careful not to presume with our own judgments.

Moses was unquestionably one of the wisest and most discerning men to ever walk the earth. Even so, he was disqualified from leading Israel into the Promised Land because he misused the rod of authority that had been given to him. The Lord told him to speak to the rock and bring forth water, but *in his own anger* he struck the rock (see Numbers 20:7-12). He represented God as being angry when He was not.

Anyone else could probably have gotten away with that, but because of the authority Moses carried and the close relationship he had with the Lord, he was held to a much higher level of responsibility. If we are going to walk in the higher realms of authority, we will be held to a higher level of accountability. The things that you can get away with in the Outer Court will get you killed in the Holy Place. Therefore, the more authority that is entrusted to us, the more dependent on Him we must be, and the less dependent on ourselves.

For the love of Christ controls us, having concluded this, that one died for all, therefore all died;

and He died for all, that they who live should no longer live for themselves, but for Him who died and rose again on their behalf.

Therefore from now on we recognize no man according to the flesh; even though we have known Christ according to the flesh, yet now we know Him thus no longer (II Corinthians 5:14-16).

This is our goal: to be controlled by the love of Christ, to no longer live for ourselves but for Him, to see all men with His eyes, to hear them with His ears, and to know them with His heart.

SEVEN

Counterfeit Spiritual Authority

The counterfeit of true spiritual authority is what the Bible calls witchcraft. There are many forms of this evil, from the manipulation used in certain sales techniques to the black magic practiced by cults and demon worshipers. Those who are called to walk in spiritual authority are often tempted to succumb to this evil by engaging in manipulation, hype and other forms of soul power. These practices can be the beginning of a fall into some of the most powerful forms of bondage and spiritual deception.

Because I have covered this in depth in my booklet entitled *Overcoming Witchcraft,* we will only address the most basic issues of counterfeit authority here.

Self-Promotion Leads to Divination

The over-promotion of one's gift is a sure sign that there are probably other destructive problems in that person's ministry, even if the gift is real. A prophet who promotes himself will usually end up crossing the line between revelation and divination. Prophetic experiences are not necessarily an indication of one's maturity or importance. Mature prophets seek an intimate relationship with the Lord, not influence with people.

We are exhorted to **"earnestly desire spiritual gifts,"** so it is clearly not wrong to seek spiritual experiences if we are doing so for the right reasons. However, if we are seeking such experiences out of selfish motives, we can open ourselves to receiving them from the wrong source.

This is not to conclude that our motives must be perfect before we can be used by God. Evidence that we are seeking spiritual gifts out of selfish motives will usually be found in one thing—*striving*. If one is truly called as a prophet, revelation will come without striving. An apple tree does not worry about how many apples it is going to pump out each day; if it is a real apple tree, apples will come effortlessly.

As the Lord warned (and I will continue to repeat), **"He who speaks from himself seeks his own glory; but He who is seeking the glory of the one who sent Him, He is true, and there is no unrighteousness in Him" (John 7:18).** Nothing will more quickly destroy a prophetic ministry, or any other ministry, than self-seeking, self-promotion or self-preservation.

That is why learning to deal with rejection is mandatory if we are to walk in a true ministry. Rejection is an opportunity to grow in grace and die a little more to ambition, pride and other motives which will so quickly color our revelation. If we embrace rejection as the discipline of the Lord, we will grow in grace and love. If we rebel against this discipline, we will actually be in danger of falling into witchcraft.

Every bit of influence that we gain through self-promotion will someday become a snare to us. All of the money or other resources that we raise through self-promotion will actually become a stumbling block to our ability to walk in the ministry we have been called to. Whatever is gained by striving and self-promotion will have to be sustained by the same. That will keep us from walking in the true authority God has for us.

Manipulation and hype are deadly enemies, not only to the prophetic ministry, but to *any* ministry. Those who understand true ministry and true spiritual authority will not want one bit of influence that God does not give to them.

True Authority or Witchcraft?

Those who receive their authority, recognition or satisfaction from men will, like King Saul, end up in the witch's house. Paul named witchcraft as one of the works of the flesh (see Galatians 5:20), which is where it begins, but it will end up being demonic if we do not repent. That is why Samuel warned Saul that **"rebellion is as the sin of witchcraft" (I Samuel 15:23 KJV).**

When one in spiritual authority rebels against the Holy Spirit, the void will be filled by the counterfeit spiritual authority of witchcraft. This may begin as the simple reliance upon hype and soul power to manipulate those one seeks to control. Without repentance, it can end up in the most diabolical forms of presumption and rebellion, as we see in the life of King Saul. When Saul at the end of his life killed the true priests of the Lord and had a witch conduct a seance for him, it was but the natural conclusion of a life marked by character flaws and wrong choices.

Spiritual authority is a dangerous occupation. If we are wise, we will follow David's example: not *seeking* a position of spiritual authority and not even taking one which is offered until we are certain that God has placed us in it. One of the most frequent phrases attributed to David was that he *"inquired of the LORD"* (e.g., see I Samuel 30:8). On the few occasions when David made a major decision without inquiring of the Lord, the consequences were devastating.

Making major decisions that affect God's people without even consulting Him must be one of the highest forms of presumption and pride. The higher a position of authority is, the more dangerous it is, and the more people who are affected by our decisions. True spiritual authority is not an honor to be sought; it is a burden to be carried. Those who seek authority usually do not know what they are asking for.

Even though he lived a thousand years before the age of grace, David knew grace possibly as well as anyone who has lived in this age. Yet he made mistakes which cost thousands of lives. It was probably because Solomon had observed this in his father that the one thing he desired was wisdom to rule over God's people (see I Kings 3). Anyone called to a position of leadership in the church must take this same posture of absolute dependence on God's wisdom.

Even if we are not in a position of spiritual authority, presumption can kill us. And if we are in a position of authority, it can also hurt many others as well. The gift of a word of knowledge may carry more excitement, but those who are called to walk in spiritual authority would do well to seek the gift of a word of *wisdom* even more than words of knowledge.

Humility Is a Safety Net

Those who attain prominence before humility *will fall*. **"God is opposed to the proud, but gives grace to the humble" (James 4:6).** Therefore, if we have wisdom, we will seek humility before position. True authority is based upon the grace of God, and the more authority we walk in, the more grace we need. True spiritual authority is not position; it is grace. Counterfeit spiritual authority stands on its position instead of grace. The highest spiritual authority, Jesus, used His position to lay down His life. He commanded those who would come after Him to take up their crosses and do the same.

There is a simple factor that distinguishes false prophets from the genuine ones. False prophets use their gifts and use other people for their own ends, in order to build up their own influence or ministry. True prophets use their gifts in a self-sacrificing way, for the love of Christ and the sake of His people. Self-seeking, self-promotion and self-preservation are the most destructive forces in ministry. Like King Saul, even if we have been anointed by God, we nevertheless can fall into witchcraft if these forces gain control of us.

Not only must those in leadership be wary of using witchcraft, they must also be aware that they will be the primary target of those who do. It is an enemy we must watch for, both from within and without; either way, it is extremely subtle. This form of sorcery is seldom what we call black magic, but is usually a form of "white witchcraft." This includes well-meaning people who have fallen to subtle forms of manipulation to gain influence because they do not have the confidence to be straightforward.

One prominent form of white witchcraft in many "full gospel" streams is often referred to as "charismatic witchcraft." This is not meant to reflect on the Charismatic Movement but rather on human charisma as the source of one's influence. This possibly has done more damage to full gospel movements than any other single factor.

Pseudo spirituality attempts to gain influence or control by wearing a super-spiritual mask. This is a source of many false prophecies, dreams and visions that can ultimately destroy or neutralize a church, or else cause the leaders to overreact and despise prophecy altogether. The people using this form of witchcraft will almost always think that they have the mind of the Lord and that the leadership is in rebellion.

Summary

I honestly do not think I have ever met a person in ministry, including prophetic ministry, who has not been guilty of some form of manipulation. I personally spent several years trying to cast out "Jezebel spirits" by using a control spirit on them! The apostle Paul listed witchcraft (or sorcery) as a work of the flesh because it is inherent in the fallen nature of man.

The tendency to engage in counterfeit spiritual authority is something we must all overcome. The beginning of our deliverance is simply to recognize what these forms of manipulation really are—sin. If we are going to have a valid ministry and walk in true spiritual authority, we must be delivered from this corruption.

The degree to which we get free from the tendency to manipulate will likely be the degree to which we are entrusted with the true power and gifts of the Lord. If we want to know the authentic power of God, we must get rid of all the other props and learn to lean only on our Beloved.

EIGHT

The Eyes Must Be Single

In Isaiah 29:10, the prophets are called the **"eyes."** That is the function of prophets—to be the eyes of the body of Christ. They are to provide vision so the church may go forward without stumbling, staying on the path that she has been called to walk. While it may be possible for a blind person to stay on the path, the journey will at best be much more difficult and dangerous, not to mention slow.

Many blind people have done a remarkable job of adjusting to their blindness. They learn to trust their other senses more, and often live very productive lives. However, you probably could not find a blind person anywhere in the world who would not prefer to have his sight.

Likewise, many churches have adjusted to not having the prophetic ministry operating, and are still quite productive. Even so, how much more productive would they be if they had the benefit of a functioning prophetic ministry? How much less would they trip over unforeseen obstacles or get blind-sided by the enemy? With how much more resolve and speed could they move along their appointed course? Without question, being able to see makes almost everything we do much easier.

Groping and Stumbling

Until the prophets have taken their rightful place in the ministry, the church will continue to grope, stumble and be subject to unnecessary difficulties and dangers. As the Lord said in Luke 11:34 (KJV), **"The light of the body is the eye: therefore when thine eye is *single*, thy whole body also is *full of light*."**

We should not settle for anything less than having the whole body full of light. We must also understand that this requires the eye to be **"single,"** or in unity. Isaiah 52:8 (NKJV) foretells the coming prophetic unity: **"Your watchmen shall lift up their voices, with their voices they shall sing *together*; for *they shall see eye to eye* [together] when the LORD brings back Zion."**

It would be hard to walk if one of your eyes focused on one thing and the other eye focused on something else. Although the many prophetic voices of today are often in conflict with each other, we can trust Isaiah's word that it will not always be that way.

The emerging prophetic ministry is maturing quickly, and it seems to be coming into unity much faster than the church at large. Prophets are gathering in various places and learning to walk together. This is encouraging, but the groundwork for single vision must be laid on an individual basis. We must each address the things that can blur or obscure our vision.

A Covenant with Our Eyes

First, if we are going to function as the eyes of the body, we must be careful how we use our own eyes. Job showed great wisdom in this: **"I have made a covenant with my eyes; how then could I gaze at a virgin?" (Job 31:1)** Job made a covenant with his eyes not to look upon something that would cause him to stumble. If our eye is single, fixed upon the Lord, our whole body will be full of light.

We can let either light or darkness into our soul through our eyes. If we are going to function as eyes for the Lord's body, we must give our eyes to Him, to be used only for His holy purposes. We must not let darkness into our soul through what we allow ourselves to look at. Lust is one of the primary destroyers of prophetic vision. Lust is selfishness in its basest form—the exact opposite of the nature of the Lord, whom we are seeking to emulate.

In Ephesians 1:18-19 Paul said:

I pray that the eyes of your heart may be enlightened, so that you may know what is the hope of His calling, what are the riches of the glory of His inheritance in the saints,

and what is the surpassing greatness of His power toward us who believe. These are in accordance with the working of the strength of His might.

To be prophetic, we must have the eyes of our *hearts* opened, not the eyes of our minds. The primary way that this happens is when we focus upon the Lord. That means beholding *His calling,* not just our own; the glory of *His inheritance,* not just our inheritance; and the surpassing greatness of *His power,* not our own abilities. We will only have true prophetic vision to the degree that we are looking through His eyes.

The Eyes of Our Hearts

We must also see more clearly with the eyes of our heart than we do with our physical eyes. What we see in the spiritual realm must be more real to us than what we see in the natural realm. Abraham was a prophet, and a great example of one whose vision in his heart was more powerful than what he could see with his natural eyes. He left the greatest culture on earth because he was looking for the city that God was building. He saw into the future, and lived by that vision just as if it were present reality. As the Lord Jesus confirmed, **"Your father Abraham rejoiced to** *see My day,* **and he saw it and was glad" (John 8:56).**

Because Abraham had seen the day of the Lord and the resurrection, he didn't balk at the Lord's command to sacrifice his son Isaac. He knew that his son was a type of the coming Messiah and that, like the Messiah, Isaac would be raised from the dead if necessary. This was confirmed in Hebrews 11:19: **"He considered that God is able to raise men even from the dead; from which he also received him [Isaac] back as a type."** Abraham was not living for the temporary realm, but for eternity. This is the calling of all believers, but it is a particularly essential foundation for all who would be prophetic.

To be prophetic, we must live in a different realm. We must see people not just as they are, but as they are called to be. We cannot just see the church in her present state, but must see her as she is called to become. We must often see the things that are not as though they are (Romans 4:17), and prophesy the reality of God's future plan and purpose.

The "Dry Bones" Test

Every true prophet must pass the test of Ezekiel 37. What do we see in the present valley of dry bones? Those without vision will only see death. The true prophet can see in even the driest bones an exceedingly great army, and will prophesy life to those bones.

Coming into true unity will not happen just by our getting together, but only as we are all beholding the One who holds all things together **"by the word of His power" (Hebrews 1:3).** Anyone can see Babylon, but who can see the majestic city God is building? That requires prophetic vision, seeing beyond the way things are, to the One in whom everything in heaven and earth will be summed up.

PART III

NINE

Growing In Spiritual Sensitivity

Paul Cain is a man with extraordinary prophetic gifts. One of these gifts that has particularly impressed me is the way he can be led by the Holy Spirit to specific places, such as a person's residence, without having any prior knowledge of where he must go. He has been accurately led to "divine appointments" even in cities with millions of people.

When I first saw Paul do this, I determined to try it myself. On several occasions now, the Lord has led me to places for which I had no directions. But I must confess that many *more* times I have gotten hopelessly lost, even when trying to do this on the country roads of North Carolina. When that has happened, I have had to keep in mind that Paul Cain has been maturing in his giftings for almost 50 years.

As I continue to seek the Lord for such leadings, I do become more and more sensitive to His guidance. My hope is to one day be so sensitive to the Spirit that I can be led by

Him to a specific address anywhere in the world. I am not doing this as a game, but because when I watched Paul, I was convicted that I would eventually need this same level of sensitivity to the Lord's leading. Now is the time for me to begin growing in this sensitivity, not after I am thrust into pressing circumstances.

When we are mature, the Lord does not have to lead us around by the hand anymore; He is able to *send* us. He wants us to have His judgment and wisdom so that we make the same decisions that He would make. At the same time, we must always be sensitive to His voice and His supernatural gifts of the Spirit, such as words of wisdom and words of knowledge.

When I am flying over or passing through a city, I often pray in the Spirit for that city and ask the Lord for the interpretation. As the interpretation comes, I then know what the Spirit is praying for that city and I am able to become of one mind with Him. This is how I often receive revelation concerning spiritual strongholds or special gifts and callings on the church in a city. I also do this when I pray for individuals or ministries.

Tools, Not Toys

The gifts of the Spirit are not toys; they are tools for building His church. The Holy Spirit is *holy* and we must treat Him and His gifts with reverence. At the same time, we are commanded to *"Desire earnestly* **spiritual gifts, but** *especially* **that [we] may prophesy"** **(I Corinthians 14:1).** In the days to come, we are going to need all of the spiritual wisdom, knowledge and revelation possible to accomplish the Lord's purposes, and sometimes just to survive. Now is the time for us to mature in their use.

As King David exhorted: **"Let everyone who is godly pray to Thee in a time when Thou mayest be found; surely in a flood of great waters they shall not reach Him" (Psalm 32:6).** Now is the time for us to build our houses on the rock of both hearing and doing His words. We are foolish if we wait until the storm comes before we start building (see Matthew 7:24-27).

On the day of Pentecost, Peter was compelled to quote a passage from Joel about the last days, in which increasing revelation was promised:

> **"And it shall be in the last days," God says, "That I will pour forth of My Spirit upon all mankind; and your sons and your daughters** *shall prophesy, and your young men shall see visions, and your old men shall dream dreams"* **(Acts 2:17).**

One of the surest signs of a true outpouring of the Holy Spirit is an increase in the number and intensity of prophecies, visions and dreams. When the Lord pours out

His Spirit, He increases His communication with us. Prophecies, visions and dreams are ways in which the God who is *Spirit* communicates with us who are *flesh*.

Why then, if the Lord is trying to tell us something, does He not just speak loudly and clearly enough for us to hear Him? Why does He give dreams and visions that are so hard to interpret? Basically, it is because our ways are not His ways (see Isaiah 55:8-9). He is not going to change to comply with our ways; we are going to have to change to comply with His ways if there is going to be communication between us.

In the language of the Spirit, a picture (i.e., a vision) really is worth a thousand words. The Lord is not only trying to reach our minds; He is trying to reach our hearts. He is not just trying to tell us *what* He is doing, He wants us to see *why* He is doing it. When His communication comes in dreams or visions that require interpretation, it keeps us seeking Him and dependent on Him.

Missing the Interpretation

Many who are growing in prophetic revelation have genuine visions or dreams, but then arrive at faulty interpretations. This often leads to misunderstandings about what the Lord is saying, and then to erroneous predictions.

The New Testament prophet Agabus is a good example of how one who is a mature and respected prophet can err because of a wrong assumption in his interpretation. Taking Paul's belt, he bound his own hands and feet and testified, **"In this way the Jews at Jerusalem will bind the man who owns this belt and deliver him into the hands of the Gentiles" (Acts 21:11).**

Although Agabus was *generally* correct about this prophetic warning, things did not unfold *exactly* as he predicted. Paul was actually bound by the Gentiles who had delivered him from the Jews (see Acts 21:27-36). Agabus had likely seen that Paul was going to enrage the Jews and then had seen him bound and in the hands of the Gentiles. He made an assumption about *how* this was going to happen.

It is unlikely that Paul sat in the Roman barracks fuming and calling Agabus a false prophet because he got a few of the details mixed up. Agabus had been right about the overall outcome, and Paul was likely very thankful for the warning concerning what he was about to go through.

We would all spare ourselves confusion, and sometimes serious problems, if we would learn to only share exactly what we are shown in visions and dreams, and not add our own assumptions. Usually the Lord is trying to just give a general revelation. There is often pressure to get more specific in order to verify a word or to prove our own ministry by making it more spectacular. This is presumption, and it will work to destroy the credibility of our ministry rather than to affirm it.

Many young, maturing prophets have made devastating mistakes by assuming that a revelation they received concerned something that had *already* happened instead of something that was *going to* happen or vice versa. I know a man who once received a clear and specific revelation concerning a pastor he had never met being in an adulterous affair. He even received the name of the woman who was involved, which indeed turned out to be the name of a woman that this pastor was becoming dangerously fond of. The prophet assumed that the affair had already happened, when the Lord actually sent the revelation as a warning of an impending trap of the enemy. Only great grace and humility on the part of the prophet and the pastor allowed this misinterpretation to become a penetrating lesson instead of a stumbling block.

The proper timing of events is often one of the most difficult aspects of the prophetic for me to discern. I often see a specific incident in a person's life, but I do not know if it is something that happened in the past, in the present, or that is going to happen in the future. I have learned that it is just as important to share what I do *not* know as what I actually see.

One prophet I have ministered with has grown in his sensitivity to timing to the degree that he is able to consistently give the year and month in which incidents have happened, or those in the future will happen—and I have never seen him miss. Not only do we each have our own gifts, we also each have limitations that we must recognize and live within. This is designed by the Lord to make us need each other, and is a good reason why we should normally only prophesy when there are other prophets present who can judge the revelation.

TEN

Levels Of Revelation

It is important that we understand the various levels of prophetic revelation. These range from mere impressions to being caught up into the third heaven as the apostle Paul was.

Impressions

Most of what is called "prophecy" today is on the lowest level of prophetic revelation, which is the impression level. These are general revelations that *we* have to put words to. Personally, I do not add the addendum "thus saith the Lord" to what is in fact an impression that I have expressed in my own words. The word of the Lord is precious, and the last thing I want to do is put my words in His mouth.

If something is truly the word of the Lord, it will accomplish the purpose for which He sent it, even without the bombastic embellishment we may think it needs. It is probable that we actually have done more to *devalue* our prophetic currency by overusing "thus saith the Lord" than by anything else. In fact, it is debatable whether we *ever* need to include such a statement in our prophecies today. The reason biblical prophets used this phrase was to distinguish between the Lord's words and purported messages from the many other gods of the day, all of which had their own "prophets."

Many of the "prophecies" today are in fact our own exhortations. These may well be the mind of the Lord, but are expressed in our own words. Often these impressions from the Lord get tainted by everything from our pet doctrines to how much caffeine we've had. We might be trusted with far more authority and higher levels of revelation if we start calling impressions just what they are, and do not so freely misuse those precious words "thus saith the Lord."

Visions

The next level of prophetic revelation is a vision. Visions can also come on several levels, ranging from those you see with the eyes of your heart to "open" visions which are like watching a movie screen.

When I pray for individuals, I usually see a vision with the eyes of my heart. These are so gentle I must be patient and be at peace to see them. Some of these I can interpret when I understand the biblical symbolism in which they come. For example, when I pray for someone who is called as a teacher,

I usually see rain over them. Rain is often symbolic of teaching in Scripture, as Moses said, **"Let my teaching drop as the rain"** **(Deuteronomy 32:2).** I may see feet being shod which tells me that one is an evangelist called to go forth with the gospel of peace.

Silver usually speaks of redemption. Sarah, Abraham's wife, was redeemed with silver. As a type of Christ, Joseph was sold by his brothers for silver. In the wilderness, the Israelites were required to each give a half shekel of silver for their redemption, and Jesus was sold for silver in order to redeem us. I may see the hand of the Lord offering silver to someone He is calling to salvation. I have also seen a silver band around the head of those whose mind He is seeking to redeem.

Most of the symbolism used in visions is established in Scripture, but not all of it is. The symbolism not derived from biblical usage is usually something relevant to the person or situation for whom the revelation is meant.

Once when I was ministering to a man I had never seen before, I saw a vision of him digging in a dry place and finding nothing. I then saw a large oil derrick not far away. This man got in it, and after going a short distance, he dug and hit a gusher. The vision meant nothing to me, but it meant a great deal to him. He had once been in the oil business but was at that time trying to plant a church. The vision said to him that he was not using the right tools or digging in the right place, all of which was true.

On another occasion I was praying for a young woman and saw her baking pies. The first one looked dry and stale, but I saw the Lord telling her to serve it, which she did. I then saw her bake another pie that turned out to be one of the most beautiful and appetizing pies I have ever seen. I did not know it, but this woman really enjoyed baking pies and had recently baked two pies exactly like I described. Then the interpretation came. She felt that the word and ministry she had was dry and stale, and she was feeling too ashamed to share it. The Lord was telling her to be faithful and give what she had; then He was going to give her something far greater to serve.

Once while I was speaking at a conference, I looked down and saw a vision concerning a young man on the front row. In the vision, he was cleaning toilets and then raising the dead. I felt compelled to stop my message and share the vision with him. Though I had no idea what the vision meant, I saw that it impacted the young man. Later, he shared with me that in obedience to the Lord he had left the ministry in order to become a church janitor. Having recently cleaned the filthiest toilet he had ever seen, he had sunk into a deep depression, feeling forgotten and abandoned by God. Then the Lord spoke to him and said that if he would be faithful as a janitor, he would one day raise the dead. My vision confirming this was obviously a great encouragement to him.

Revelations that appear meaningless to us may often be a loud roar from heaven to those who receive the word. Occasionally we will receive a vision that does not initially mean anything to the person it concerns, but later it may mean a great deal. If they do not mean anything to the person when they are shared, we must be patient and not start speculating about the interpretation; that is what often muddies the waters of prophetic interpretation. If it is truly God's word, He will verify it at the proper time.

Open Visions

"Open visions" are a higher form of revelation than the gentle visions we see with the eyes of our hearts. These are vivid and distinct, and are given in such a way that we cannot miss what the Lord is saying. An example of this type of vision is found regarding Cornelius, the centurion, who **"*clearly* saw in a vision an angel of God" (Acts 10:3)**. This revelation was so clear that Cornelius carried on a conversation with the angel in the vision. This level of revelation is usually infrequent, and used by the Lord to communicate matters of great importance, such as He did here in using Cornelius to open the door of faith to the Gentiles.

Although the Lord generally reserves these high levels of revelation for conveying extremely important messages, this is not always the case. I know a few people who move in this higher realm frequently, and they even receive clear and specific revelations concerning seemingly mundane issues. The Lord is sovereign, and He often departs from the spiritual principles we try to set for Him. Usually this is because even those who are the most spiritual still see **"in part"** and **"through a glass, darkly" (I Corinthians 13:9, 12 KJV).** Even so, we must share what we see, realizing that our understanding is limited.

Dreams

Dreams are also a common form of revelation. Like visions, dreams can have different levels of clarity and revelation. Some are gentle nudges from the Lord; others are bold and direct. Some are simply from the pizza you had last night!

Most of our dreams are nothing more than random, meaningless accumulations of impressions from our activities during the day. These may in some way reflect our mental state, but are in no way a message from the Lord. If you are left only with a vague feeling that a dream might have been from God, it probably wasn't. The dreams which come from Him are usually easy to tell, even if we do not immediately know what they mean.

Trances

What is probably the next highest form of revelation is the one used by the Lord to tell Peter that he was to go to Cornelius' house: **"he fell into a *trance"* (Acts 10:10).** The best way I can describe a trance is that it is like having a dream while you're awake. All of a sudden, you are caught up into a vision that is so real it seems as though you are literally there, but you are wide awake and aware of when you left and when you return.

These experiences were quite frequent both in the Old and the New Testaments. John's revelation on the Isle of Patmos would fall into this category, as would many of Ezekiel's experiences when he was caught away and brought to Jerusalem. Paul was caught up into the third heaven so that he did not know if he was in the body or out of it (II Corinthians 12:2-4).

Peter's vision of the sheet filled with unclean animals is a good biblical example of a directive revelation (see Acts 10). The vision was given to help overcome Peter's natural resistance to God's leading that he should visit the Gentile household of Cornelius. It helped him make a critical decision and resulted in a major stronghold being brought down. This episode resulted in a difficult theological change of a basic doctrine then held by the church. Until that time, the gospel had only been offered to the Jews. Even going to the house of a Gentile was a very hard thing for a religious Jew such as Peter to do.

There is a precaution we must observe whenever a prophetic revelation is given to alter a doctrine. Peter was right to immediately respond to the Holy Spirit and go to the house of Cornelius, but then it was also right for him to submit this revelation to the council in Jerusalem for confirmation. When the Holy Spirit gives such directives, we must allow believers the freedom to respond and obey Him as individuals. However, before this change is accepted as a new doctrinal position for the church, it must be submitted to the elders and confirmed by the Scriptures.

Since Peter was an apostle, some might argue that only those in leadership should have the authority to respond to such directives. But later, in Acts 11:19-21, we see some unnamed believers taking a similar initiative and preaching to the Gentiles at Antioch. If the church is going to walk by the leading of the Holy Spirit, we must learn to balance two principles that are frequently in tension: the freedom of individuals to take their own initiative in response to revelation from the Lord; and the need for proper submission to the authority God has instituted in the church. This is not an easy balance, and few have been able to walk in it, but it is essential for the vitality and protection of the church.

Other Prophetic Experiences

There are other kinds of high-level prophetic experiences, such as hearing the audible voice of the Lord, being visited by angels, or even being visited by the Lord Jesus Himself (see Acts 23:11). Because we are entering a time of a great outpouring of the Holy Spirit, all of these experiences are becoming more common.

Even though we are commanded to **"earnestly desire spiritual gifts,"** it is not always wise to seek spiritual experiences. There is a tendency for many to feel that if they just had one of these experiences—such as seeing an angel or being caught up into the third heaven like Paul—they would not have the problems they now are experiencing with walking by faith. That is probably not true. Satan saw the glory of the Lord, dwelt in His presence, and often appeared before His throne, yet he still fell.

These experiences can undoubtedly help us in our mission or they would not be given, but we do not need experiences as much as we need *grace*. Christians who become experience-oriented are invariably the weakest and most unstable in the faith. Those who build their faith on revelations and visions are foolish indeed (see Colossians 2:18-19). Such occurrences are *tools* for building, but they themselves are not the building, nor are they even the main tools.

While I believe it is wrong to desire spiritual experiences for the wrong reasons, it is certainly not wrong to pursue them for the right reasons. In fact, the desire you have may well be the Lord's way of preparing you for such experiences. I have had almost every type of prophetic experience discussed here, but I only *asked* for two of them. The others just happened to me because I needed them for a message or mission that I was given.

The Lord's Audible Voice

One day I asked the Lord to let me hear His audible voice. Some of my friends had often heard the Lord speak in this way, but though I frequently heard His voice in my spirit, I had never heard Him speak audibly before. When I asked, He said that He would. So I sat down in a chair and braced myself, thinking how great it was going to be. When He spoke, He said one of the most personal, beautiful and loving things He had ever said to me—but it is impossible to describe the terror I felt!

The Lord's voice was not loud; I do not think it even rattled the windows. Yet there was such depth and endless power in those words that I felt like a mere atom standing before the sun. I actually heard eternity, and it was almost more than this frail human body could take. I immediately quit criticizing the Israelites for asking Moses to convey God's messages to them so that they would not have to hear His voice directly. I deeply treasure what He said to me, but it took me quite awhile to want to hear His audible voice again—and I am quite content for Him to decide when that should be.

Angels

I have seen angels on a number of occasions, and each time the experience was comforting and encouraging. But I am confident of one thing: No one who has really seen an angel will presume to command one! As my friend Francis Frangipane likes to say, "These guys are *not* the Gerber babies with wings that many artists have portrayed them to be!" Even Jesus, who was made **"a little lower than the angels"** while on earth (see Hebrews 2:5-9 KJV), did not presume to command them. He only said that if He *asked His Father*, He would send them (Matthew 26:53).

Of course, Jesus is now much higher than the angels, and we too will one day judge them. Even so, we are foolish and vain to try and command things we do not understand. How do we know if we need a legion of angels or just one big one? Like Jesus, we would do well to just ask our Father to take care of such things for now.

Not only is there danger in the presumption of *commanding* angels, as if we were their boss, there is also danger in *worshiping* them. John was apparently the disciple who had the most intimate relationship with Jesus, and after

Jesus ascended, John walked with Him in the Spirit until old age. Yet, even after having such a deep relationship with Jesus and then seeing Him in His glorified form at the beginning of the book of Revelation, John later in the vision falls down to worship an *angel*! (Revelation 22:8-9)

If that could happen to John, it can certainly happen to us. We should not be giving our attention to angels, but to the Lord. The Lord gave very little revelation in Scripture concerning angels, because He does not want our attention on them. They are ministering spirits who are devoted to the ministry and protection of the saints (Hebrews 1:14), but they are under the *Lord's* command, and He knows how best to use them.

The early church was obviously quite familiar with angelic appearances. When Peter was released from prison, it was easier for those praying for him to believe that his angel was standing at the gate than it was for them to believe that Peter had been released (see Acts 12). There are a number of occasions when angels intervened on behalf of believers, but the church did not make a big deal out of it, and always gave the Lord the glory rather than His angels. Let us do the same.

Revelation or Divination?

There is a fine line between revelation and divination. Presumption will cause us to cross that line. Satan's counterfeit of the trance is one of the more popular occult practices. When we need supernatural experiences, the Lord will give them to us. But instead of seeking experiences, we must seek to be *worshipers*, growing in grace and the knowledge of Jesus Christ and firmly established upon sound doctrine. There is more joy and ecstasy in true worship than in most of the spiritual experiences, except for those that somehow bring us into His presence or let us behold a measure of His glory.

The Lord did great miracles in front of the multitudes, but it seems that He saved His best for the eyes of a few, such as walking on water. It has been my experience that the Lord is the same way with prophecy. I have seen some of the clearest and most specific revelations given during a meeting, only to have no one responding to it. After we have been made to look foolish and the meeting is over, the people for whom the word was intended will often come forward, usually saying they "weren't sure" that it was for them! For a long time I thought the Lord did this just to humble us, but it does seem that He likes to perform the most special miracles on an intimate, personal basis with the person He is touching.

The Lord is not performing miracles or giving us prophetic revelation so that He can impress people (or so that *we* can). He could stop the sun or move the mountains if that were His purpose. Miracles and revelations are given to accomplish something for His people. They are but the means to an end, not the goal itself. If revelation and power become ends in themselves, they will be perverted. They are the gifts of the Holy Spirit; let us treat Him as holy.

The apostle John laid his head on the Lord's breast, where he could hear His heartbeat (John 13:23). That place is still available. It is better to know the ways of the Lord than to just see His acts. As wonderful as it is to know the Lord's mind or see what He is doing, it is better still to be so intimate with Him that we know His heartbeat, so that our hearts might beat in unison with His. When we have been established in this place, He will be able to trust us with much greater revelation and power.

ELEVEN

Interpreting Dreams And Visions

Because both the book of Joel and the book of Acts affirm that one of the primary ways that the Lord will be speaking to His people in the last days will be through dreams and visions, it is imperative that we be able to interpret them accurately. Presently, this is an area where the prophetic ministry tends to make a lot of mistakes.

Common Stumbling Blocks

The first step in gaining greater accuracy in the interpretation of dreams and visions requires taking a look at the factors that seem to be the most frequent stumbling blocks.

#1 - Presumption

It is easy to start assuming that because we understand some biblical symbolism we can therefore use simple formulas for interpreting divine revelation. However, even our attempts to interpret the Scriptures should make it clear that symbolism can actually be contradictory. For example, in most places in the Bible, a serpent represents Satan. But Moses also used the serpent to represent the *Messiah* when God told him to raise it up on the staff to provide for the people's healing (Numbers 21:6-9).

The Lord seems to purposely provide us with conflicting symbolism in order to keep us dependent on Him for the interpretation of any revelation that He gives us. Goats often represent the demonic, but in Moses' use of "the scapegoat," it was obviously another prophecy of the Messiah (see Leviticus 16). We must prayerfully seek the Lord for understanding, regardless of how obvious an interpretation may seem. True interpretations must come by a revelation of the Holy Spirit.

#2 - Looking Only from Our Personal, Present Perspective

In this present life there are few times when we do not have something weighing heavily on our hearts. It is easy to assume that any revelation we receive pertains to our own present concerns. We need to beware of this tendency to try and fit the interpretation to our own situation, when very often the Lord is speaking about something entirely different.

God views everything from the perspective of eternity. He sees things from the vantage point of His entire plan and purpose. To accurately interpret what He is saying to us, we must see from His perspective rather than from our own.

#3 - Seeing Through Fear Rather Than Faith

If we are going to see from the Lord's perspective, we must understand that He is not sitting in heaven wringing His hands and worrying about things. He has already seen the end of all things, and He is in total control of anything that He wants to control. The gift of discernment is required for interpretation, but many fall into the trap of substituting *suspicion* for true discernment. This is rooted in fear, which will *always* distort our perception.

True discernment can only operate in godly love, the perfect love that casts out all fear (I John 4:18). **"God is love" (I John 4:8),** and if we are going to see with His eyes, we must see through the eyes of love. God certainly is not afraid of the enemy, and anything that is colored by fear is a distortion of true spiritual vision.

#4 - Majoring on Minors

The first calling of the prophetic ministry is to prepare the way for the King, not to look for the enemy. When we are primarily focused on looking for the enemy, a very serious distortion of our vision takes place. It is noteworthy that apparently not a single one of today's so-called "watchman ministries" has ever foreseen the Lord coming in a new movement and begun to prepare the way for Him. This should be an obvious alarm about the character of those ministries. Looking more for the enemy than for the Lord will put us in jeopardy of becoming the "faultfinders" that Jude wrote about (Jude 16 NIV). By sowing fear and division, some self-appointed "watchmen" have done far more damage to the church than have the cults they are so concerned about.

The Lord commended the church of Thyatira for *not* knowing the deep things of Satan (Revelations 2:24). We will be changed into the image of what we are beholding (II Corinthians 3:18). If we are beholding the glory of the Lord, we will be changed into His image. If we are spending more time looking at the enemy, we will be changed into *his* image and will be used as an accuser of the brethren.

This is why many of the heresy hunters become so mean-spirited, easily departing from biblical teachings on bringing correction in the church, when they themselves claim to be protectors of the Scriptures. We must be vigilant and able to quickly recognize the enemy, but we must also be careful not to hastily call someone the enemy until we are sure of what we see. It is not wise to trust the vision of anyone who does not see the Lord and what He is doing much more prominently than they see the enemy.

#5 - Prejudices

Prejudices can be cultural or religious. If we are prone to be prejudiced toward a race, sex, age group, denomination or movement, it can seriously warp what we are seeing. Jesus came to save the whole world, and in Christ **"There is neither**

Jew nor Greek, there is neither slave nor free man, there is neither male nor female; for you are all one in Christ Jesus" (Galatians 3:28). Prejudices against any such group is a dangerous spiritual flaw that the enemy will easily be able to exploit if we do not repent and ask the Lord to change our heart.

#6 - Having Prejudicial Doctrines

Of course we must be committed to sound doctrine. However, the Lord does not give prophecies to verify doctrines—He gave the Bible for that. Those who use prophecy to establish doctrines are in danger of serious diversions. This misuse of prophetic gifts can be found at the root of most cults.

Exhorting believers either to maintain or return to the recognized precepts of the faith is one of the functions of the prophetic ministry. But prophetic revelation is not the proper vehicle to *establish* the precepts. We should not trust those who attempt to use prophecy to promote their "pet doctrines" or other agendas.

It has been the downfall of many anointed prophetic men and women to try and become teachers. There are some who are gifted as both prophets and teachers, but they are usually those who are in preparation for an apostolic commission. When one who is just a prophet tries to be a teacher, or one who is just a teacher tries to be a prophet, the consequences have often been devastating.

#7 - Rejection

As we have addressed at length, prophets are often rejected, but they must never let rejection grip their spirit. If we are overly affected by rejection, we will always be in jeopardy of compromising the ministry. Dwelling on past rejections will keep us self-centered instead of Christ-centered, which will obviously cause a distortion in our vision. Rejection, if not healed, will usually turn into the next serious problem that distorts interpretation: bitterness.

#8 - Bitterness

The priests in the Old Testament could not have scabs (Leviticus 21:20). Scabs are little, unhealed wounds. One who has unhealed wounds will be overly sensitive and hard to touch. When spiritual wounds are not healed, they can become infected and turn into bitterness. The writer of Hebrews warns that such a root of bitterness will defile many (Hebrews 12:15).

One prophetic friend of mine was once told by the Lord that the only difference between a spiritual sheep dog that protects the sheep, and a wolf that devours them, is that the wolf has unhealed wounds. Most false prophets were called as prophets of the Lord. Many of the grumblers and faultfinders that Jude warned the church about are gifted prophets and watchmen who have become bitter and critical.

Learning to forgive is basic Christianity; whenever we fail to forgive, we are departing from the path of life.

#9 - Rebellion

Rebellion is usually rooted in either rejection or self-will, both of which can be deadly to the prophetic ministry. Extreme rebellion is usually evidenced by the declaration that we will not submit to men, but only to God. This is the twisted flip side of the fear of man. Since God usually speaks and works through people, such a mentality is a profound deception. The true fear of God that is not subject to the fear of man is free to properly recognize, honor and submit to all who are anointed by God.

There can be a fine line between revelation and divination. Because **"rebellion is as the sin of divination [witchcraft], and insubordination is as iniquity and idolatry" (I Samuel 15:23),** we must be diligent to guard our hearts against rebellion or insubordination. This can be a very large open door for the enemy to enter through, just as we see in the life of King Saul.

#10 - Unsanctified Mercy

Unsanctified mercy is having mercy for the things that God is judging. Intercessors often take on the burdens of the people, but prophets must take on the burden of the Lord. Very often these are in conflict. It was for this reason that Peter received one of the most frightening rebukes in Scripture,

"Get behind Me, Satan! You are a stumbling block to Me; *for you are not setting your mind on God's interests, but man's"* **(Matthew 16:23).**

Jesus responded not to human need, but only to what He saw the Father doing. He had compassion for human needs, but compassion did not dictate His actions; the Father alone did. Those who are ruled by human compassion instead of by the Holy Spirit will often be used by the enemy in one of his primary strategies for wearing down the saints—infiltrating the church with "false brethren" who consume most of the leadership's time and energy, while producing little fruit or change.

#11 - The "Party Spirit"

When we derive our recognition from a single organization, there will usually be pressure to prophesy the "party line." This makes it very difficult not to compromise prophetic integrity. All true authority for ministry comes from the Lord, not the church, and certainly not just one segment of the church. Ordination papers are the equivalent of letters of recommendation that were used by the first-century church (II Corinthians 3:1), and are helpful for verifying ministries. It is also proper that we should be submitted to a local church, and sometimes a movement of churches, but we must always understand that true authority comes from God.

If we are to represent the Lord properly to those we serve, we must guard against, and sometimes even stand against, this party spirit. If unchecked, it will pervert prophetic integrity and damage the church or movement that we are called to serve. The high priest carried the stones of *all* the tribes on his heart (in the breast plate), and if we are to walk in the high calling, we must ultimately carry the whole church on our heart, not just one congregation, denomination or movement.

#12 - Failing to Submit to the Body

Regardless of whether an unwillingness to submit to the body of Christ is caused by rebellion, rejection or just negligence, it will be costly. I have found that even those who have extraordinary gifts of interpretation often have a difficult time interpreting their *own* dreams and visions. The Lord limits His ministries this way, because He wants everyone to need the rest of the body.

We can also be much more objective in interpreting other people's revelation than we can when interpreting our own. The prophetic people that I know who consistently hear from the Lord on the highest levels rarely hear from the Lord about important matters in their own lives, but are often dependent on others to give them a prophetic word when they need it.

Every ministry that I know, including some outstanding prophets, have a major blind spot in their life which makes them dependent on others to see for them in certain matters. If we do not learn to work together and trust each other's special gifts, we will be regularly hit by the enemy in those blind spots.

#13 - Lust

Lust is one of the primary destroyers of prophetic vision. In Isaiah 29:10, prophets are called the "eyes." Prophets are called to function as the eyes of the body of Christ. As the Lord explained, **"The light of the body is the eye: therefore when thine eye is *single*, thy whole body also is full of light"** **(Luke 11:34 KJV).** This speaks not only of unity and singleness of vision, but also of the fact that if we are going to use our eyes for the Lord, we must use them for Him alone. Only in this way will we be **"full of light."**

Job declared, **"I have made a *covenant with my eyes*; how then could I gaze at a virgin?" (Job 31:1)** Job made a covenant with his eyes not to look upon that which would cause him to stumble. If we desire prophetic vision, we would do well to make this same covenant: that our eyes belong to the Lord and we will not use them for evil. Lust is rooted in selfishness, the exact opposite of the nature of the Lord and the nature of true prophetic ministry.

#14 - Using Natural Eyes Instead of the "Eyes of Our Heart"

Prophetic revelation comes from the Spirit. We must therefore be careful not to let ourselves be overly influenced by what we may know in the natural. If we have natural knowledge concerning something that we have been asked to seek the Lord about prophetically, we should always let it be known that we have that knowledge in the natural. This is crucial in order to preserve prophetic integrity.

We must also be careful not to let things that appear one way in the natural affect our spiritual perception, especially as it relates to people. For example, the people who outwardly seem to be doing well are often hurting the most on the inside. People put up facades, and those with the strongest outward appearances are often the weakest on the inside.

Being prophetic requires much more than natural perceptiveness. Occasionally the Lord may anoint a perception in the natural and use it for revelation, but more often than not, *natural appearances will lead to a wrong conclusion!* This happened to the prophet Samuel. Even though it was said of him that the Lord let none of his words fail (I Samuel 3:19), he received a strong rebuke from the Lord over this very issue of trusting in natural appearances: **"Do not look at his *appearance* or at the height of his stature, because I have rejected him; for God sees not as man sees,** for man looks at the *outward appearance*, but the LORD looks at the *heart*" (I Samuel 16:7). God does not see as we see, and if we are going to be used as His eyes for the body, we must learn this lesson well.

Understanding Spiritual Symbolism

It cannot be overemphasized that prophecy is a spiritual gift, and is not a skill that can be learned by mastering certain principles or formulas. Yet, because prophetic dreams and visions do involve symbolism, understanding symbolism is important to the gift of interpretation. There are biblical symbols that *usually* mean the same thing in prophetic revelation.

Gold usually speaks of the divine nature because it does not tarnish. Copper speaks of the human nature because it has a likeness to gold, but easily corrodes. Silver usually speaks of redemption. The color blue speaks of the realm of the Spirit because it is the color of the sky, or what is referred to as "the heavens." Red often speaks of sacrifice because it is the color of blood. Purple is the royal color, or color of authority, because it is a combination of blue and red, and spiritual authority is based upon both divine revelation and sacrifice.

A dry river bed in a dream or vision will usually relate to a spiritual movement or denomination that is no longer anointed, for a dry river bed is a place where the waters *used* to flow but no longer do. Flies often speak of lies, because Satan is called Beelzebub (Matthew 12:24), which means "lord of the flies," and he is **"the father of lies" (John 8:44).** Flies also breed on garbage or waste that has not been properly disposed of, which is the source of many of the enemy's lies that he uses against the church.

This is but a very superficial explanation of how some symbols can be interpreted. A future book will address the subject in much greater depth.

TWELVE

The Secrets Of
The Heart

When Paul discussed the gift of prophecy in I Corinthians 14:25, he said that by it **"the secrets of [the] heart are disclosed."** I do not believe we should use this one text to make a doctrine that all New Testament prophecy must disclose the secrets of the hearts of those to whom it is given. However, this can be an important aspect of prophecy, causing people to declare that God is truly among us.

I frequently receive prophetic words from people I do not know. Many of these prophecies seek to dictate the course of my entire ministry or move me to become a part of an outreach or ministry that would consume a massive amount of my time and energy.

I ordinarily do not pay any attention to such directive prophecies from strangers unless there is an aspect of the word that discloses something in my heart that no one could know about unless the Lord showed them. Even that will not cause me to necessarily accept the entire prophecy, because I realize that immature people can get something valid from the Lord and then add a lot of their own opinion to it. But this aspect of disclosing something in my heart does at least get my attention enough that I will seriously pray about the rest of the prophecy.

I do have a number of friends whose prophetic revelation I have grown to have great confidence in, but I still judge every word they give to me. I believe that there is only One who is perfect, and anyone else can make a mistake. That is why we are exhorted to judge prophecy. I find it helpful that even my trusted friends—whose words I will always seriously consider—generally have aspects in their prophetic words for me that disclose a secret of my heart that they had no way of knowing.

For example, one friend told me the details of an open vision I had received, then gave me the interpretation. I had just received the vision, and had not even had the time to tell anyone when this man called and described the vision to me. Had he called me with a word concerning something that he already knew about in the natural, his word obviously would not have made the same impression on me. I would possibly have considered it the counsel of a brother, but not necessarily a word of prophecy.

When the Lord reveals the secrets of our hearts through prophecy, it causes His word to go deeper into our hearts. Most of us can quote the verse about the Lord knowing every hair on our head (Matthew 10:30), but when a prophetic word reveals something that only God could know about us, that knowledge is transferred from our minds to our hearts.

When the Lord reveals the secrets of our heart, it lets us know experientially that we truly have no secrets from Him. He is with us in every circumstance and in every thought. When this is demonstrated to us through a prophetic word or experience, it results in a much greater intimacy and fellowship with the Lord.

Our Hearts, Not Our Minds

When we think of having the secrets of our hearts revealed, our first reaction may be to recoil in horror. It is true that many dark and evil thoughts pass through our minds, probably each day. But what passes through our minds is not necessarily what is in our hearts. Our minds are, at times, subject to impressions from the enemy, which may cause us to feel guilty. But the thoughts were really not our own—they were being impressed upon us.

Our bodies also make many impressions on our minds. If you ever go through caffeine withdrawal or suffer from sleep deprivation, you will probably think evil things about anyone who annoys you—but these thoughts are not really your *heart*. The Lord has no interest in embarrassing us or making our secret sins public. He uses the gifts of prophecy and words of knowledge to impress upon our hearts, not just our minds, how intimate He really is with us. When that knowledge gets into our hearts, it will usually cause us to deal with any secret sins without God even having to address them.

One of the reasons the Lord uses prophecy to reveal the secrets of our hearts is to impress upon us the reality of His calling in our lives. Every calling is going to be met with difficulties and trials, but we can endure these problems much more easily when we begin with a profound knowledge that the Lord has truly called us to the task.

The ultimate purpose of the Lord is not just to change our minds about things, but to change our hearts. He looks on people's hearts, not just their mind or actions. The heart is the "innermost being." The Lord therefore usually speaks to the heart. Our innermost being usually is veiled to others, and often even to ourselves. Prophecy that touches these secrets can also set us free to do things we otherwise would not have had the confidence to do. Over the past few years I have heard thousands of testimonies of how personal prophecy accomplished just such a thing in a person's life, leading them into their ultimate calling and purpose.

Confirmation Only?

I have heard many people teach that prophecy should always be just a confirmation of something the Lord has already spoken to us. But I do not think that this view can be biblically established. In fact, it seems that the opposite is much more frequent in the Scriptures. In most cases, prophecies were given in the Bible because people were going the wrong way and needed *correction,* not confirmation. However, sometimes the Lord does give prophecies as a confirmation. He sometimes even repeats them, but this should not be made into a principle.

One area that confirmation is often helpful is in relation to our calling or ministry. Again, this is not true for everyone, and we do not need the same degree of confirmation for every calling. The general principle is that the more specific and dramatic the confirmation is, the more difficult the task will be. This is not an indication of how *important* the task will be, but only how *difficult.*

Nevertheless, many of the most effective men and women of God in history accomplished their purpose with little or no prophetic confirmation to their ministry. Others, meanwhile, received repeated prophetic confirmations and words of encouragement along their course, even though they may not have recognized the words as being "prophetic."

We must understand that the Lord calls us to walk by faith, because true faith keeps us dependent upon Him. Along with even the most dramatic and specific confirmations, He will always leave some room for faith. Many desire a specific word from the Lord about every calling or task they are inclined to do, but it is not in their best interest for the Lord to do this.

Prophetic Addiction

The Lord does not want us to become addicted to prophetic words! Often it is far more important for us to grow in faith and in wisdom than to have prophetic directives. When the Lord does speak to us specifically, it is usually because of the difficulties we are going to face—we will need the extra confirmation in order to make it!

Receiving continuous words from the Lord to give us help and direction is not a sign of maturity, but of immaturity. Toddlers need continuous directives and oversight, but as the child matures he should need less of this input. The same is true of us spiritually. The apostolic teams in the Bible were not led around by the hand—they were sent by God as mature messengers. They had the mind of the Lord and, except in rare circumstances, were able to make decisions in accordance with the Lord's will without the need for prophetic words or confirmations.

For Paul's first missionary journey, he received a specific prophetic commission. For his second mission, which many consider to have been his most fruitful, there was no specific word to go. He just felt that he should return to check on the churches that he had established. When we are young, we do need to be led by the hand. When we mature, we can be *sent* by God. The mature apostle did not need or seek a specific revelation for everything he was to do; he made decisions as a trusted ambassador who had the mind of Christ. He was obviously open to receive prophetic direction, but he was not dependent on it.

When Paul received a specific prophetic word from Agabus concerning the difficulties he was to face when he got to Jerusalem, these revelations were not meant to turn him from the course, as some of those giving the words seemed to think, but rather to help prepare him for what he had to face. The nature of this prophecy to Paul was not directive, but it simply imparted knowledge concerning future events to help prepare him for what he would endure. Even though his fellow workers took these words as directives and instructed Paul not to go, the apostle knew differently and, like the Lord Jesus, he remained resolute in facing his trials in Jerusalem.

Directive Revelation

In Paul's ministry we also have a good example of a specific, *directive* revelation, which was the vision he had about going to Macedonia (Acts 16:9-30). This revelation helped him make a critical decision, as well as prepare him for difficulties. Timing is important in ministry, and Macedonia was ready for him—but it obviously was not on Paul's agenda until the Lord gave him this vision. Soon after arriving in Macedonia, Paul was beaten and cast into prison. Having the clear, directive vision to remember during these difficulties probably enabled Paul and Silas to praise the Lord even in their chains, thus resulting in the jailer's conversion and the beginning of a great work.

Most of those in ministry today who are open to prophetic revelation have similar testimonies of the Lord's specific guidance in their lives. Jesus would not be the Head of the body if He could not direct it. He often does this through prophecies, words of knowledge, words of wisdom, dreams and visions. Spiritual maturity is coming to the place where we are completely free for the Lord to speak to us and direct us in any way that He chooses, but are also wise enough to do what we should even when He does not give us specific direction.

Many confuse this latter aspect of spiritual maturity with presumption. They feel that if they do anything that God has not specifically told them to do, they are just "doing their own thing" and asking God to bless it. Of course, there are many ministries and churches that are run that way, seldom seeking the Lord's counsel and almost completely unable to hear His directives. But there is a level of spiritual maturity where the Lord appreciates our *initiative*.

We are the same way with our own children. If I mention to my daughter that she should witness to one of her friends and she does it, I might be satisfied, but if she did it on her *own initiative* I would be much more pleased. My daughter's obedience is important to me, but when she does the right thing on her own initiative, I know it is truly in her heart. That will please me far more than her mere obedience.

The same is true with the Lord. He will always be the King of Kings and Lord of Lords. We will always be under His authority. But He is trying to prepare us to rule *with* Him, not just under Him. It is pleasing for Him to see us doing the right thing without Him having to give us every little direction.

The Scriptures testify that the last days will bring some of the greatest troubles the world has ever known. During these times we will need personal prophecy, words of knowledge, words of wisdom and discerning of spirits possibly more than the church has ever needed them before. We will need them to take our stand and war against the schemes of the enemy. We will also need them for greater accuracy and efficiency in ministry. Having the most accurate doctrines will not help us if we are not in the Lord's will.

Heeding God's Signs

Signs and wonders are not toys, they are tools. Spiritual signs, like physical signs, are meant to direct us. When there is a demonstration of the Spirit that becomes widespread in the church, we need to ask the Lord what He is trying to say to us with it.

Throughout church history there have been recorded incidents of the phenomenon that is popularly called today "being slain in the Spirit." Even though some may be faking the experience, many are clearly not. The Holy Spirit really does move upon some people, knocking them to the floor and sometimes pinning them there for hours.

But God is not "slaying people" just for our entertainment—there is an important message in this demonstration of the Spirit. *The Lord is not just trying to change us—He's trying to kill us!* If we are going to be used by the Holy Spirit, our old man must die. If we are going to walk in the Holy Spirit, we must be dead to ourselves and dead to this world.

In the early 1970s, another interesting spiritual phenomenon started sweeping through much of the church. There was a great anointing for what was called "leg lengthening." Many people have back problems caused by one leg being slightly shorter than the other, and often the source of the problem is not really a leg, but a hip that is out of adjustment. Multitudes, including myself, who had legs that were not equal in length or hips that were out of adjustment were prayed for and instantly healed.

Leg lengthening was great fun, and some of the miracles were spectacular to watch. Even so, many missed the message that the Lord was trying to convey with this special "sign": *The body of Christ was out of balance.* He wanted to give us the same anointing for correcting the spiritual imbalances as He did the physical ones.

Today we are seeing an increasingly specific manifestation of the gift of a word of knowledge. A few years ago, it was awesome when a minister said that there were 10 people present in a meeting who had a heart problem, and 10 people would stand up for prayer and be healed. This kind of thing is still wonderful to see, but it is no longer spectacular. There are a number of people in ministry today who can, at times, even call out the 10 people by name and give details about their problems, such as how long they have had the condition, how many operations they have had, and other facts that no one but God would know.

These supernatural manifestations are not a case of one-upmanship, *they are signs from the Lord!* As we proceed toward the end of the age, we must dramatically grow in our ability to hear specific and accurate words from God.

Yesterday's standard of obedience to the Spirit is not sufficient for today. The whole church must come to the place where we can hear the Lord more clearly and accurately than ever before.

PART
IV

THIRTEEN

Prophecy And Spiritual Warfare

Paul exhorted Timothy, **"This command I entrust to you, Timothy, my son,** *in* **accordance with the** *prophecies previously made concerning you,* **that** *by them* **you may fight the good fight" (I Timothy 1:18).** Timothy was told that the personal prophecies made concerning him would help him fight the enemy. This reflects an aspect of personal prophecy which will become increasingly important as we approach the close of this age.

I have been given a number of personal prophecies that have greatly strengthened me and helped me to withstand the attacks of the enemy. In some cases these had to do with promises from God that the enemy was attempting to steal. On one occasion God spoke to me about a certain promise that He was going to fulfill in my life very soon. Then two different people called me with a prophecy that the enemy was coming to steal a promise that God had given to me.

I took the warning seriously and prepared for the attack. It came within a month and was far more intense than I was even expecting, but I had been strengthened enough to hold my ground. The attack soon crumbled, and I received the fulfillment of God's promise a few months later. Without those warnings, I do not think I would have been able to endure the intensity of the enemy's attack.

A Major Onslaught

One of the greatest attacks of my life unfolded over a 10-year period, and a personal prophecy actually delivered me from it. Before I became a Christian, I was basically a materialist, which means I did not believe in the supernatural at all. When some friends of mine claimed that they could make demons manifest with their incantations, I just thought they were taking too many drugs. Then one night I went to one of their meetings and witnessed these demons visibly manifesting themselves. It was not only a terrible shock, but I knew that whatever they were, they were evil and I wanted nothing to do with them.

Then these demons started appearing to me every few days, and they would tell me that I was theirs and could not escape from them. When I told a friend about these experiences, she immediately told me to "use the name of Jesus on them." So the next time these demons appeared,

I used the name of Jesus and, sure enough, they fled, seemingly terrified. After that, I decided to buy a Bible and find out about this Jesus whose name could drive away such evil beings.

This led to my conversion. At first I really thought that the whole supernatural world was very weird, but I knew that Jesus was "good weird" and the other was "bad weird." That was about the limit of my theology at the time (which enabled me to lead far more people to the Lord than I have since my theology became more "proper").

After my conversion, I sought the Lord passionately. I studied the Bible for about 40 hours a week, making a living on part-time jobs so that I would have more time for study. I gradually quit the vices I had been involved in, which were many. The more I studied, the more grateful I was for my good fortune at having come to know about Jesus.

But then the demons started appearing again, telling me that I was not the Lord's—I was theirs. I would "use His name on them" and they would leave for a while, but their words continued to hound me. My joy at learning about Jesus turned into a deep depression over the possibility that I wasn't really His.

As my depression increased, the demons started appearing more frequently. Soon I could not sleep, and wanted to die. Never in my life had I been suicidal, but I was getting close at that time. I could not bear the thought of not truly being the Lord's, nor of belonging to the evil one.

One night I woke up feeling the presence of someone in the room. I rolled over quickly, expecting to see one of the demons, but this time it was the Lord. He stood elevated above the floor in the corner of my room. He did not say anything; He just looked at me. When I looked into His face, all I saw was love. I knew that He loved me and that I was His. He started to walk toward me and then passed through the wall, just above my head.

This entire experience lasted no more than a minute, but it erased all the fears that those demons had put in me. The depression was gone, and the demons did not come back for ten years.

Revelations from Hell

I entered the ministry and tried to pastor a church, but I failed miserably. I became so caught up in ministry that I almost forgot my relationship with the Lord. Since I was a pilot, I decided to take a corporate flying job that would give me the spare time to seek the Lord and reestablish a personal relationship with Him.

I was dealing with a lot of guilt because of the problems my immaturity in ministry had caused for so many of the people I had tried to pastor. Then a group of these people asked me to return to the city where I had pastored so I could meet with them and hear a "major revelation" they had received. I returned and met with them, and was informed of their "revelation": I was a false prophet.

In painting me as a false prophet, the people claimed to have words of knowledge about secret sins in my life—but their "revelations" were simply not true, and I knew that they were speaking the same words that the demons had spoken years earlier. Yet I was feeling like such a failure that it occurred to me that the demons might be right.

As I flew home, I pondered the Scripture that every tree is known by its fruit (see Matthew 7:15-20). I then started looking at the fruit of my own ministry and it certainly did not look good. The only fruit that I could see was injury and heartache inflicted upon God's children. From my depressed point of view, I lost sight of any good fruit that had come from my life and ministry. I forgot about the people I had led to the Lord, many of whom were still walking with Him and doing well. I could only see the bad.

The wave of depression that swept over me was greater than I had experienced for 10 years. I'm quite sure that if my wife had not been in the plane with me, I would have purposely crashed it into the ground. This was not normal depression—it was supernatural and there was no way I could live with it much longer. I desperately wanted to die.

163

When Julie and I arrived at our apartment, I noticed the truck of our good friend, Doc, who was a surgeon and also our present pastor. He had been waiting there for us, and as soon as we arrived he jumped out of his truck. Without even greeting us, he said, "I don't know what you were told in Raleigh (the city I had just returned from), but that word was not from God!"

The night before, Doc and the whole church had been caught up in the presence of the Lord. They received only one word from Him—that I had been given a word from the enemy in Raleigh, and they were to warn me immediately not to receive it. Doc had sat patiently outside our apartment, determined to wait until I returned.

I knew there was no way that Doc or anyone else in the church could have known about my experience, because I had not even told my wife what the people said. As he shared what the Lord had spoken about me at the meeting the previous night, the depression immediately lifted. I sincerely believe my life was saved by the church's sensitivity to the Spirit of God.

Avoiding a "Black Hole"

Years later, the same people who had been used in this attack against me began coming to some of our conferences. I was genuinely glad to see them, because I know we do not war against flesh and blood, but against principalities and powers. I had always felt that these people were just used by the enemy because of the open door he had through their wounds. We had some good fellowship at the conferences, but then I began to feel uncomfortable about some things that I observed. For one thing, I saw them attempting to get close to a prophetic friend of mine by appealing to his wounds and loneliness—always a bad sign.

As I was debating whether the Lord had brought these people back into my life to address some of the old problems, or whether this was just the beginning of another attack from them, Mahesh Chavda came over to share a word with me. He said that the enemy was sending an attack against me from the east (Raleigh is due east of us), and that the attack was coming in the form of trying to draw me into an effort to heal the wounds of the past. Mahesh sensed that this was just a "black hole" that they had created by refusing to forgive.

Although I felt Mahesh's word was extremely clear, the Lord spoke to me about a sign that would confirm this even further, and it came to pass. Immediately the root of bitterness in these people surfaced, and it was clear that this had in fact been an attempt of the enemy to draw me into their "black hole."

Would I ever be open to these people again? Yes. I do not believe in giving up on anyone. I consider them brothers and sisters, even though I believe they are deceived in some areas and have allowed a root of bitterness into their lives. They are not beyond God's power to redeem and deliver, and I pray to have the grace never to give up on any living human being.

So why did I not just stick it out with these people until they were delivered? Even though to some that might have seemed the "spiritual" thing to do, the Lord had made it clear through the prophetic word that I was not to do this. It could have distracted me for years, or even permanently. I do pray for them, but I know that I am not the one the Lord has called to lead them to healing.

Protective Prophecies

One of the greatest attacks against the church in the last days is going to come from false brethren. These are not merely false shepherds, false prophets, or false teachers, but false brethren. They are being sent to steal the children's bread, consuming 90% of the pastor's time, energy and resources without ever really changing or producing fruit.

As watchmen and shepherds, we must learn to spot these spiritual traps and avoid them. False brethren are "black holes" of self-centeredness and self-pity, who will steal the children's bread if we do not recognize them and refuse to continue ministering to those who do not produce fruit in keeping with their professed repentance.

Prophecy can be used in spiritual warfare in numerous other ways, such as warnings in dreams and visions. This is how Joseph was warned to take the baby Jesus to Egypt in order to escape from Herod. The wise men were warned in this way not to return to Jerusalem. One prophetic friend of mine was told what to say to an IRS agent to avoid being audited. He was not hiding anything, but the enemy was trying to tie up his ministry for months in an extensive audit, which he was happy to avoid.

Bob Jones has called me a number of times to share a revelation concerning an attack on one of my children, and he then tells me how to pray and break the attack off of them. He and Paul Cain have also discerned and helped to thwart specific attacks coming upon our staff. Sometimes we are too close to people to see them accurately, and words from those outside of the family or ministry can really help.

One of the purposes of prophecy is to help the church prepare for whatever is coming in the future. We need to be prepared as much for revival as we are for conflict. As we get closer to the end, it will become increasingly important to have dependable prophetic ministries serving the entire body of Christ.

I am not taking the time in this book to go into much detail about my own prophetic experiences, because I am planning to follow this book with one devoted almost exclusively to that. Even so, the following chapter shares an experience that I think will be helpful.

FOURTEEN

When Prophecy And History Meet

Having a clear word from the Lord can give us the tenacity to stand or the courage to make difficult decisions while under great stress. When we have a clear prophetic commission to ministry, such as Paul and Barnabas received at Antioch (Acts 13:1-4), we are more likely to hold our course through the difficulties and opposition that will surely come.

There are also misuses and misinterpretations of the prophetic that can cause us problems if we do not handle them properly. Several times I have received a prophetic revelation concerning something the Lord was going to do, but when I attempted to bring it to pass, I failed. I then watched as someone else came along and fulfilled the word. I finally began to understand that many of the words and visions I was receiving were for *other people* to accomplish.

Next, I went to the other extreme, thinking that every word I received was for someone else to fulfill—and I started

169

missing some of what the Lord wanted to do through *me*. How can we know the difference? And how can we discern the important factor of timing? It takes maturity, and the only way to get maturity is through experience, which often comes through making mistakes!

Tragically, very few seem willing to continue on their course after experiencing failure. However, just as the Lord gave the keys of the kingdom to the disciple who seemed the most prone to make mistakes (see Matthew 16:13-23), those who make the most mistakes are often the ones used by God to bring the greatest spiritual advances. Even so, there is another way to discern the nuances of the prophetic gift that can help us avoid many of our blunders. That is, we need to seek the gift of a word of wisdom as much as we seek the more spectacular gifts.

As Solomon understood:

> **By wisdom a house is built,**
> **And by understanding it is established;**
>
> **And by knowledge the rooms are filled**
> **With all precious and pleasant riches (Proverbs 24:3-4).**

Here we see that knowledge can fill the house, but wisdom builds it. The prophetic gifts and ministry are not just to use for gathering people. In fact, it is a grave mistake to try and gather people or build our ministry around a certain gift. We must only gather people to *Jesus*, and only build upon the relationship that we have with Him. The gifts are all given to draw people closer to Him, not to us.

Our goal must always be to build the people up into a temple for the Lord. This requires the gift of a word of wisdom. All the gifts of the Spirit are supernatural, and so is this gift. Having a word of wisdom is much more than just being intelligent or having common sense. This gift is a wisdom beyond human ability.

Supernatural words of wisdom may not be quite as impressive as words of knowledge, but to those who understand the church's purpose and destiny, the words of wisdom can be far more valuable. What good does it do to gather people, if they are not being built into the temple? Most congregations are presently nothing more than great piles of living stones. They need to be fitted together, which is the special work of this gift.

A Prophetic Story

The following is the story of how I have prophetically entered into some of the purposes for which I have been called. I am sharing this not only to illustrate the practical benefits of the prophetic ministry, but also to point out some of the mistakes I have made so you can avoid them.

In 1981, while my wife, Julie, and I were attending a very small congregation in Jackson, Mississippi, the Lord gave me a vision for a teaching center and prophetic sanctuary. Because my attempts to fulfill some of the visions I had received in the past had failed, I assumed that my vision for a teaching center was for this congregation that we were attending. But when I shared it with the leadership, they looked at me as if I were speaking a foreign language.

Meanwhile, the Lord was continuing to unfold to me different aspects of this vision. He began teaching me about the coming apostolic authority, yet warned that until the prophets and teachers learned to worship Him together as they did at Antioch, apostolic authority could not be fully released. Soon this was a deep passion of my heart, but the more I tried to share it with that little congregation, the more trouble it caused. Finally I came to understand that it was not for them, but for me.

I then proceeded to make another mistake with this vision. I purchased some property and began landscaping it and planning for the teaching center. One day when I was out on the tractor working and praying, I was telling the Lord how much I loved the land and how much I was looking forward to seeing the teaching center take shape. Immediately I felt His presence in a powerful way, and He began to speak to me. He said that the land was nice, but that it was not the place that He had chosen for the center!

I was stunned. The Lord then began speaking to me about going to "the mountains of North Carolina" and returning to full-time ministry. When He had first given me the vision of a teaching center and prophetic sanctuary, I had not even inquired about the place or the timing, but had just charged ahead with it! The price I paid for this lack of wisdom was very high and very painful.

I looked at the land I had been working on so diligently, and immediately lost my heart for it. At the time, I had a thriving business, but I quickly lost my heart for that too, because one of my main reasons for going into business was to help pay for the teaching center. However, the business was now so big and complex that it didn't seem possible to get out of it easily.

The Lord told me that the publishing ministry He was going to give me would one day be much bigger than the aviation business I had then. He said to put the business on the altar and He would take care of it. He did. It went up in flames on that altar before I could even figure out what was happening.

Timely Words from God

Even after this, I was still a bit hesitant about entering the ministry. I was such a failure the first time I tried to be a pastor, I never wanted to try that again. I still had some good business prospects, which would give me the time to do a lot of ministry too, so I started to pursue them.

Then, in the same week, two people from different parts of the country approached me with the same prophetic word. The word was that if I did not return to the ministry then, He was going to give my commission to someone else. These two people did not know each other, and I knew that their words were from the Lord. I immediately decided to drop all of my business endeavors, go into the ministry full-time, and move to North Carolina.

By September 1987 I had written **There Were Two Trees in the Garden** and was starting to receive requests to speak in churches. I accepted a few of these invitations, and ended up speaking at churches in a number of different states.

Since I had not read Christian magazines nor watched Christian television for years, I really had no idea what was happening in the body of Christ. I felt that by visiting a variety of churches I would begin to gain a sense of this. I did, and I was shocked and deeply disappointed by what I found. I was also surprised by my lack of anointing on this initial trip. I knew that I did not have the answers that people needed for the confusion and disorientation I saw everywhere.

After I returned from this ministry trip, I went to my study to seek the Lord's direction in my life and pray about the condition of the body of Christ. Immediately I fell into what I now understand was a trance. For the next two and a half days, I was shown an unfolding of events that was far greater than anything I had ever considered previously.

What I saw in this experience became known as *A Vision of the Harvest.* Although the vision did not give me any answers about what I was to do next, it did give me a new resolve to commit my whole life to being a part of God's last-day ministry. I did not know how the church was going to get from where she was to where I saw her in this vision, but the vision gave me great confidence that it would happen.

North Carolina

I knew that I was called to the mountains of North Carolina, so I started looking for a place there. A longtime friend, Harry Bizzell, offered to let us stay at his retreat center in Charlotte until we found our place in the mountains. Before we got to Charlotte, the Lord showed me that I was going to stay there for a time, because He was going to bless us in the city as well as in the country (see Deuteronomy 28:3).

God did bless us in the city. Even though we had left a beautiful home and the nice land we had in Mississippi in order to live in a little 900-square-foot cottage, we were happier than we had been in years.

Soon I had more ministry invitations than I could accept. I also began meeting men of God who had a similar vision of the great harvest that was coming. James Robison and T.D. and Dudley Hall were some of the first. James told me that I needed to meet a man named Jack Deere. While James was speaking to me about Jack, the Spirit was speaking in my other ear, telling me that I would indeed meet Jack and he would be one of the great teachers in the last-day church.

A few weeks later, I met Mike Bickle in Minnesota. He then came to North Carolina to visit, bringing with him Jack Deere and Bob Jones. I had prayed about Jack and already felt that I knew him, but Bob was a shock! Before we had even shaken hands, he began telling me things about myself and my family that he could not have known without revelation from God.

What Bob Jones shared with me that day was in more detail and depth than I had ever before witnessed in a prophetic gift. I assumed at first that he was receiving all the words spontaneously, but Mike later explained that Bob had been having dreams about me for several years. Even so, it was a level of the prophetic gift that was greater than I had ever witnessed. As amazed as I was, this turned out to be only a very small beginning compared to the prophetic events to come.

Bob's words to me were not only encouraging, but they gave me an understanding that has been an invaluable help. Just one of the insights that he shared with me that day, concerning the enemy's strategy to thwart my ministry, has helped to keep me on course as much as any understanding that I have ever received. Bob established the credibility of that insight with exact knowledge of events that showed how the enemy had used the same tactics against me in the past.

Bob then gave me some details about how Satan would employ this strategy in the future, and it came to pass. However, this time when the enemy came to attack, I was waiting! For the first time, I learned how much more fun it is to ambush the enemy than it is to get ambushed by him!

A few weeks later, Bob called me and asked if I knew that I was going to the mountains. I said that I did. Bob then told me of a dream he had in which he had seen the exact place where I was going, and he began to describe it in detail. He said that it had old oak trees and white rocks on the boundaries. He saw a large rock-face mountain above it, and a beacon on another peak. There was a building in the center with a red roof. He was also shown that it was 40 miles from the Tennessee border and 100 miles from where we were in Charlotte. Bob said that I was going to meet a man named

Ricky Skaggs who also had a burden for the mountains and would have a part of the ministry with us there.

Although I had heard the name Ricky Skaggs and thought that there was a country music singer by that name, I was not really sure, because I rarely listen to the radio or watch television. I also thought Bob's word was probably referring to *another* Ricky Skaggs anyway. Bob just said that was the name he was given, and could add no further details. Shortly after that, I met Ricky Skaggs the country music singer, and we quickly became good friends. One of the first things Ricky shared with me was his burden for the mountain people.

Moravian Falls

Tom Hess, a friend who has an intercessory prayer ministry in Jerusalem, called and told me he had been given more than 20 plots of land in different parts of the U.S. and he was planning to give them away. He felt that he was to give the one that was in North Carolina to us. I asked where it was, and he said it was in a place called Moravian Falls. I had never heard of it, so Harry Bizzell and I got out the map and looked it up.

When Harry and I measured the distance of Moravian Falls from Tennessee, it looked like just about 40 miles. When we measured its distance from where we were in Charlotte, it looked like just about 100 miles, and that was almost the exact distance on our odometer when we later drove to see it. Sure enough, the boundaries of the land were marked with white rocks and some oak trees. Towering over it was a mountain with a rock face. On the next peak there was a radio tower with a flashing beacon. Right in the middle was an old building with a rusted red tin roof.

When Tom heard of the remarkable ways in which Moravian Falls fulfilled Bob Jones' word for us, he was sure he had found the right people to give the land to. He said that he had a three-man board that would have to approve it, but it should be no problem. Later, as I was praying about the land, I was given a direct word from the Lord not to take it with any strings attached. I saw Bob Jones again a short time later, and he said that a "spirit of anger" had been released by the enemy to come against our purpose on that land.

A few days later, Tom called and said that the board had approved giving us the land, *"with the following conditions..."* The conditions were actually favorable to us, but they were also definite strings that were being attached. I told Tom that I could not accept the offer. He later told me that he was shocked by the *anger* that arose in the men on the board when they heard I had rejected their proposal.

Even though it appeared that we might not be given this particular plot of land, we knew that Moravian Falls was the

179

place to which we were called. Julie and I decided to make an offer on a nice little house in nearby Wilkesboro, and the real estate agent said the terms we proposed were exactly what the owner wanted. The agent promised that she would call us that night with an agreement.

When the agent called, she said that when she gave our offer to the owner, an "irrational anger" came over him. She said his rage was so great that the real estate company had decided they could not represent a man like him. That sounded like a "spirit of anger" to me! I was encouraged though, because I have never seen anything of true spiritual significance accomplished without a battle, and obviously the battle was on.

Steve Thompson, who had become our administrator, then decided to research Moravian Falls. I consider the original Moravians to be possibly the purest move of God since the first century. Count Zinzendorf, the Moravian leader, has been called "the rich young ruler who said 'yes.'" Zinzendorf could have been one of the most powerful men in Europe, but he esteemed being a pastor as a higher calling and became the first nobleman in Germany to be ordained to the ministry.

Zinzendorf and a small group of friends had bound themselves in a covenant to devote their lives to sending missionaries to those who had never heard the gospel. He became the true father of modern missions (William Carey has been called "the father of modern missions," but even he pointed to the Moravians as his inspiration). The Moravians then became some of the greatest examples of sacrifice and devotion for the sake of the gospel found in the history of Christianity. Some even sold themselves into slavery in order to pay their passage to the West Indies so that they could reach the slaves there.

The Moravians are famous for their 100-year, continuous prayer meeting, which they kept going in support of their missionaries. Zinzendorf and other Moravians also wrote some of the great hymns, which became an inspiration to Charles Wesley after he and his brother, John, were both led by the Moravians into a deeper walk with the Lord.

Pursuing the Vision

All of these aspects of the Moravian movement are a basic part of our vision at MorningStar Publications and Ministries. More than any other group, the Moravians have been an inspiration for our ministry, and we were extremely excited when we started researching Moravian Falls and learned that it had actually been bought by Count Zinzendorf himself in 1750. It was a 100,000-acre plot that he purchased for use as a base for reaching the Americas. That land was called "the Wachovia tract," which means "a fruitful field." When this land was purchased, Bishop Spangenberg of the Moravian Church had it deeded "to our Lord Jesus Christ." He also prophesied that its streams would never run dry, and they never have.

We have now purchased several hundred acres in Moravian Falls. Some of it came easily, but other portions came only after serious spiritual battles. There was one 46-acre tract that we felt was the most important. Bob Jones had received a dream in which he was shown a mountain with "a pillar of fire that was made out of lightning," two streams, and a cave that the Lord told him was "the cave of Adullam where God's mighty men would gather." We could see the spiritual significance of these things, but Bob insisted that there was also a literal cave on the land that he saw.

Many months later when I drove Bob to see the 46-acre tract that we wanted to purchase, he said that it was the same land he had seen in his dream. When he pointed to where the cave should be, I told him I didn't think any cave was there. However, later that day we found out that a cave was indeed located in exactly the direction Bob had pointed.

The cave turned out to be an old iron ore mine, and we found out that the iron ore still in the mountain caused lightning to strike it just about every time a storm got close. Remembering that in Bob's dream he had seen a pillar of fire made out of lightning, I fully expected to hear that there were also two streams on it. Sure enough, when the land was being surveyed they found two streams of water coming out of that mountain.

We knew that this was a very important piece of land for us to get, but the owner did not seem very interested in selling it. He told us several times that he would call us back with a price, but soon he would not even return our calls.

One night while we were staying in Moravian Falls for a ministry team retreat, Bob Jones was awakened by the Lord very early in the morning and told to go up to our boundary marker and strike it with a staff we had given to him. When Bob struck the boundary marker, a huge demon manifested, which Bob knew had been assigned to thwart our purpose there. Bob continued striking the marker until the demon disappeared.

The very next week, the man who owned the 46-acres called and said he would like to sell it for exactly the price we felt that we should pay. Within two weeks, all the real estate deals that we had been unsuccessfully pursuing started opening up.

I have witnessed the effectiveness of many prophetic events, such as Bob striking the boundary marker or people marching around buildings. However, to use such actions as a *formula* is not prophetic—it is divination. Bob took the action he did in obedience to a specific instruction from the Lord. An angel actually woke him up and told him to do it.

When the demon manifested after Bob struck the boundary marker, we gained insight into how the enemy was seeking to thwart our work there. It has all been very helpful, but we must not make a practice out of any such things lest we start to trust in methods and formulas instead of in the Lord. That is a trap that leads to witchcraft.

Summary

Our ministry has been greatly helped by the prophetic revelations we have received, such as the ones concerning our Moravian Falls Project. However, many of the fruitful aspects of our ministry have not been based upon any prophetic leading, and these are just as much a part of what God has called us to do. It is wrong to think that God is only blessing the things that come about by a dramatic prophetic leading, while anything else is less important. We should never forget that some of the most fruitful ministries in history were undertaken with no prophetic guidance.

Dramatic prophetic revelation usually comes because of the difficulty of the task, not necessarily the importance of it. We know that the destiny of our ministry is linked to Moravian Falls, and that we will be launched into our ultimate purpose there. Perhaps our project there needed such a solid prophetic foundation because one of its primary purposes is to be a prophetic community.

However, we must not be overly dependent on prophetic guidance or we will probably end up missing the Lord. We are not called to follow prophetic ministry, but to follow Him. Prophetic ministry is but one way that He leads us. If that is the way that He has chosen in a particular case, we will miss Him if we do not listen to the prophets. But if we become overly dependent on the prophets, He may start speaking to us more through other means just to help correct our focus.

It has taken me more than 25 years of receiving various levels of prophetic revelation to begin to get a sense of both the interpretation and application of prophecy, and I still feel that I have just begun to learn these things. My hope is that as I publish more of my experiences in prophetic ministry, it will help others to grow faster and avoid having to suffer some of the setbacks that I have had.

FIFTEEN

A Foundation For True Church Life

So then you are no longer strangers and aliens, but you are fellow citizens with the saints, and are of God's household,

having been built upon *the foundation of the apostles and prophets, Christ Jesus Himself being the corner stone*,

in whom the whole building, being fitted together is growing into a holy temple in the Lord;

in whom you also are being built together into a dwelling of God in the Spirit (Ephesians 2:19-22).

No building can exist without a foundation. The foundation is what the entire building rests upon. If the foundation is removed, nothing else can stand. In I Corinthians 3:11 Paul writes, **"For no man can lay a foundation other than the one which is laid, which is Jesus Christ."**

Jesus is not just the foundation; He is the whole building. We are to grow up in all aspects into Him. All of the ministries are merely vessels through which He ministers to His church.

When Jesus started building His church, He began with the apostles and prophets. These ministries are foundational for true church life, because they are the foundation of *Jesus'* ministry as both Apostle and Prophet. He is both **"the *Apostle* and High Priest of our confession" (Hebrews 3:1)** and the *Prophet* whom the Father sent into the world (Deuteronomy 18:18-19).

We can experience many great blessings from the Lord, but we will not have true church life, the way that the Lord intended for it to be, until the apostolic and prophetic ministries are restored to the church. They are foundational for true church life, just as the text in Ephesians 2:20 states.

Rebuilding the Temple

Today we are in a time like that which was prophetically paralleled in the time of Ezra. Israel had been conquered, her people carried away to Babylon in slavery, and her land and cities made desolate. This is comparable, in many ways, to the present state of the church.

After 70 years, which represented the completed time of Israel's exile, a small remnant of the people had a vision to return and restore the temple of God in Jerusalem, which had been torn down. The church has also come to such a time. A remnant has been moved by a vision to return to the "land" of our spiritual inheritance and to restore the temple of God (the church) to its intended glory and purpose.

After the remnant returned to Jerusalem, they immediately began laying the foundation for the temple. After the foundation was completed, they held a celebration. The younger people, who had never seen the former temple, greatly rejoiced at the potential and hope they saw in this foundation. Many of the older ones, who had seen the former temple, were discouraged and wept because the new foundation did not seem to measure up to what they had previously seen (see Ezra 3:10-13).

The same is happening today. A foundation has been laid upon which the church can be rebuilt to its intended glory and prominence. But many of the older saints, who have seen a vision of what the "first temple" (the first-century church) looked like, are discouraged by what they see now.

Despite the discouragement of some in Ezra's day, the worship of this little remnant was so intense in their rejoicing after the foundation was completed that it was heard for a great distance. This stirred up the enemies of Israel, who plotted to stop the work on the temple. Finally these enemies stirred up the authorities (King Artaxerxes) and succeeded in stopping further work on the temple by force of arms.

Then work on the house of God in Jerusalem ceased, and it was stopped until the second year of the reign of Darius king of Persia.

189

WHEN the prophets, Haggai the prophet and Zechariah the son of Iddo, prophesied to the Jews who were in Judah and Jerusalem, in the name of the God of Israel who was over them,

THEN Zerubbabel the son of Shealtiel and Jeshua the son of Jozadak *arose* and *began to rebuild* the house of God which is in Jerusalem; and *the prophets of God were with them supporting them* (Ezra 4:24-5:1-2).

Here we see that the work on the temple of God ceased *until* the prophets started prophesying. This is one of the primary reasons that the Lord is again raising up the prophetic ministry—not to *do* the work, nor even to *lead* the work, but to give inspiration and assistance to those who are called to provide the leadership. Ezra gives a succinct testimony to the effectiveness of such an arrangement:

And the elders of the Jews were *successful* in building *through the prophesying* of Haggai the prophet and Zechariah the son of Iddo (Ezra 6:14).

The spiritual history of the twentieth century revolves around those who have had a vision to see the church restored to its intended glory. Like their biblical forerunners, most of those with this vision have laid a foundation, celebrated over it, and then later become discouraged, to the extent that they went off to build their own houses, leaving the temple unfinished.

The Lord is raising up a prophetic ministry to prophesy to those who are called to finish this work and to stand by them until it is completed. We can read in the books of Haggai and Zechariah the wonderful way in which this was accomplished, with prophecies so parallel to the ones being proclaimed today by the rising prophetic voices.

Confusing the Roles of Prophet and Elder

It is crucial that these roles of prophet and elder not become confused. Biblically, there were a few leaders who were also prophets, such as Moses and David, but these were exceptions. Prophets seldom held positions of authority over the people, but rather they were called to *serve* those who were in authority. Even those who anointed the kings submitted to the kings.

Historically, some of the greatest errors inflicted upon the church and some of the greatest falls from grace came when someone with a prophetic ministry started to take authority that he or she was not called to have. Both biblically and historically, we see that prophets can fall quickly, and cause many others to stumble, when they try to exceed the limits of their authority. It is also the biblical and historical testimony that leaders will stagnate or sink into idolatry if they do not have prophets supporting and encouraging them. The proper working together of both leaders and prophets is essential if the work of God is to be completed—but each must refrain from trying to do the other's job.

As stated, the prophet's function was to *encourage* the building, not *direct* it. Paul probably had to warn the Thessalonians not to despise prophetic utterances for the same reasons that many today have begun to despise prophecy: (1) The demeanor of many who give prophetic messages is hard to endure, and (2) Many who presume to speak in the name of the Lord are really ministering in the spirit of "Jezebel." Let's briefly examine both of these reasons:

1. *The demeanor of many who give prophetic messages is hard to endure.* Biblically, few prophets were "normal" people by anyone's definition of that word. They had unconventional experiences that were not common among ordinary folks, and they simply tended to be strange people. Often they were called to stand alone, or with a very few, against the sins of an entire nation.

Many today who are called as prophets have tried to take on the perceived nature of their Old Testament counterparts, which has often resulted in a distortion of their own calling and nature. True prophets are *not* by nature critical, judgmental and harsh! That which is of the Holy Spirit will have the fruit of the Spirit, which is love, joy, peace, patience, kindness, goodness, faithfulness, gentleness and self-control (Galatians 5:22-23). And as James reminds us:

> **The wisdom from above is first pure, then peaceable, gentle, reasonable, full of mercy and good fruits, unwavering, without hypocrisy. And the seed whose fruit is righteousness *is sown in peace by those who make peace* (James 3:17-18).**

If we have the Holy Spirit, we will manifest His nature. He is **"the Helper" (John 15:26 NAS).** He is not aloof, just standing back and pointing to what needs to be done, but rather He helps with the work. If we are to expound on what needs to be done, we also need to be willing to get our own hands dirty with the task.

The Holy Spirit is also **"the Comforter" (John 15:26 KJV).** Even some of the hardest biblical prophecies of impending judgment were tempered with hope and offers of reconciliation for those who repented.

The nature by which the Lord brings correction is beautifully displayed in His words to the seven churches of Revelation (see Revelation 2 and 3). He *first* praised each church for what they had done right. He then clearly and specifically told them what they were doing wrong, along with the potential consequences if they failed to repent. He left each church with a glorious promise if they took action to overcome their problems.

The Holy Spirit is sent to convict of sin, but the manner in which He does it is not in conflict with His basic nature. A prophet who is called to speak specific messages by the Spirit has as much or more responsibility to live by the fruit of the Spirit as any other Christian. If the prophet does not have the fruit of the Spirit, we have a right, and even a responsibility, to reject their message.

2. Many who presume to speak in the name of the Lord are really ministering in the spirit of "Jezebel." The Lord rebuked the church of Thyatira for tolerating the woman **"Jezebel, who calls herself a prophetess" (Revelation 2:20).** Jezebel was the wife of Ahab, the king of Israel during the time of Elijah the prophet. She was a manipulative woman who controlled the king and used him to seduce Israel into the worship of idols and foreign gods. This was happening to the church in Thyatira and has happened to many congregations since.

The "spirit of Jezebel" is most often referred to in relation to women who have this manipulating and controlling nature, but this spirit is by no means limited to women. Some of the most powerful Jezebel spirits are at work in men who call themselves prophets! The true goal of those who move by this spirit is *control*. This demon is often remarkably subtle, claiming to only want what is best for God's people. Those who operate by this spirit usually *do not* want to be in a position of leadership; they just want to control the leaders.

This controlling spirit is really not difficult to discern. While James 3:17-18 states that the true word of the Lord will come with peace, gentleness and good fruit, when someone is ministering in the spirit of Jezebel, the same words may be spoken but you will feel pressure, guilt and often confusion.

Titles

It is noteworthy that this Jezebel in Thyatira *"calls herself a prophetess."* Those I know who have the greatest prophetic anointing and gifting ordinarily do not call themselves prophets, or even like it when others call them that. One can have a gift of prophecy and not be a commissioned prophet. I have not yet met anyone who went around calling himself a prophet who had a true prophetic commission, even though he may have been gifted.

There is a place for enduring the title of prophet, or another ministry title, for the sake of helping to clarify one's function and purpose in the church. There was a time when Paul had to defend his apostleship, but he did not do it for his own recognition; he did it for the sake of the people. When someone presents their title or credentials for their own recognition, we can confidently know that there is at least the potential for serious problems with that person.

"The spirit of prophecy is the testimony of *Jesus"* (Revelation 19:10). Those who have the true Spirit of prophecy and the testimony of Jesus will not care to be known by anything but their Christlikeness. The purpose of all ministry is to manifest the sweet aroma of the knowledge of

Him in every place (II Corinthians 2:14), not to establish our own authority or prominence.

Summary

The prophetic ministry is essential for true church life, because it is the part of the body through which the Lord speaks to His people in a personal, present sense. When the Lord is speaking prophetically, there is a recognition of His presence among us that is the very essence of true church life.

True church life could be defined as the Lord actively dwelling among His people. When He is among us, He builds us and fits us together into a temple in which He can dwell. The Scriptures are clear that the prophetic ministry is essential for this to happen.

SIXTEEN

Watchmen For The Army Of God

One of the basic aspects of the prophetic ministry is to be a "watchman." Prophets in the Old Testament are often called watchmen because this was a characteristic of their ministry (e.g., see Ezekiel 3:17). As the prophetic ministry is now being restored to its proper place in the body of Christ, this part of the ministry is becoming increasingly important for us to understand and function in.

Prophets were called watchmen because they basically functioned in the spiritual realm in the same way as the literal watchmen did in the natural. The natural watchmen were stationed at posts on the walls that gave them clear visibility to watch for the coming of the king or other members of the nobility, so they could announce their coming. They were also to look for enemies and for any disorder arising within the city or camp of Israel.

These watchmen were especially trained to be able to distinguish the enemy from their Israelite brethren. Only those with the best vision and judgment were given these posts. They had to be accurate in their discernment, and could not be overly prone to sound the alarm or to request that the gates be opened. If there were too many false alarms, the people would begin to disregard them. If they were careless and let an enemy in the gate, they could jeopardize the whole city. This was a position of great responsibility, for which extraordinary accuracy and dependability were required.

The ministries given to the church can only function efficiently if they are properly related to the other ministries. Because they are all still in the process of being restored to their proper biblical place, those in the watchman ministry cannot function to full capacity until the other ministries have taken their rightful place too. However, until that time comes, we must do what we can in the place to which we have been appointed. This will in turn help to bring clarity of function to the other ministries.

There are many today who consider themselves watchmen who are obviously not called to that ministry. In some cases, these individuals are making a noble attempt to fill a void left by those who have abdicated their rightful place in this ministry. Even so, the misuse of this title has resulted in confusion regarding the watchman's role, and the rejection of it altogether by many who see it being used improperly. The answer is not to reject the ministry, but to pursue its proper functioning by those who have been called to it. This will become increasingly critical as we proceed toward the end of this age.

The Watchmen Stations

The biblical positions of the watchmen were (1) on the walls of the city (Isaiah 62:6-7), (2) walking about in the city (Song of Solomon 3:3), and (3) on the hills or in the countryside (Jeremiah 31:6). Together these can give us a good picture of the operation of this ministry.

Because the city of God is a picture of the church, the bride of the Lamb (Revelation 21:2), the watchman's role on the walls of the city would have to do with the church. This could include a local congregation or the church universal. Watchmen on the walls of the city would be in a position of elevated visibility so that they could see both outside and inside of the city. These were the ones who were trained to recognize both the enemy and their brethren from a great distance. However, they had no authority to confront either. They simply gave their information to the elders who sat in the gates. Only the elders had the authority to either command that the gates be opened or to sound the alarm.

The watchmen appointed to walk inside of the city could more closely observe the activity within. These were especially trained to make a way for the king or the nobility who were passing, or to recognize and confront disorderly or unlawful behavior by their brethren. They could apprehend violators, but they could not imprison them or impose sentences, which was solely the duty of the elders who served as judges.

The watchmen on the hills patrolled the borders and countryside. They could see either the enemy or the nobility long before they got to the city. They could distinguish their countrymen from their enemies, or from foreigners who came as traders or ambassadors. Again, they did not have the authority to call for a mobilization of the army or to let foreigners freely pass, but they communicated what they saw to the elders who had the authority.

The Lord has called spiritual watchmen today who are to serve in each of these three positions. He has some whose only purpose is to be watching within the church for the movement of the King, and to make a way for Him. These are also called to recognize and report to the elders any disorderly or unlawful behavior. There are also some who have been given a place of vision that enables them to see both inside and outside of the church. And some watchmen are called mainly to roam around as scouts in the world, able to spot such things as the rise of a new cult or a major persecution against the church.

Watching and Praying

Isaiah 62:6-7 says that the function of the watchman was not only guarding, but praying. This is crucial, because most of our discernment will come in prayer. In Ezekiel 3:17 we see that the watchman was to *hear from the Lord* and warn the people. This is where many who are called to be watchmen depart from their course. They begin looking more for the enemy than for the Lord, causing both their vision and their discernment to become distorted.

The watchman ministry is spiritual, and the place of true vision is in the spiritual realm, which is entered through prayer and worship. Prayer helps to purify what we are seeing. The prayers of the watchmen can also sometimes quiet the disorder or drive away the enemy without even having to notify the elders and sound the alarm.

The first principle of this ministry is not looking for the enemy, but being in communication with the Lord. Scriptures such as Jeremiah 6:17, Isaiah 21:5-10 and Habakkuk 2:1-3 are some of the scriptures that address this aspect of the watchman ministry.

Knowing the Times

One of the important functions of the watchman ministry—often overlooked but desperately needed—is knowing the times. We see this in Isaiah 21:11-12. You can probably remember an old movie where the watchman walked about the city and called out, "Twelve o'clock and all's well." I have met many people with prophetic gifts, but only a couple who could accurately foretell both events and the timing when they would take place. As we proceed toward the end of this age, timing will become increasingly critical in all that we do. We must pray for the Lord to raise up the last-day **"sons of Issachar, men who understood the times, with knowledge of what Israel should do" (I Chronicles 12:32).**

We would do well to ask the same question that Job asked: **"Why are *times* [of judgment - margin] not stored up by the Almighty, and why do those who know Him not see His days [timing]? Some remove the landmarks; they seize and devour flocks" (Job 24:1-2).** The rest of this passage in Job 24 reads almost like a commentary on the present condition of much of the body of Christ. When we fail to see the timing of the Lord, even our spiritual boundaries become blurred.

One of the psalmist's most desperate lamentations for his nation under siege was, **"We do not see our signs; there is no longer any prophet, nor is there any among us who knows *how long*" (Psalm 74:9).** The Lord wants His people to know *when* He is going to move, *when* judgment is coming, and *when* the enemy will come. This is an essential aspect of the prophetic ministry that must be recovered and positioned properly in the body, or we will continue to pay with unnecessary defeats and catastrophes.

Recognizing Our Sphere of Authority

The watchmen were not the elders in the gates, and they did not have the authority to either open or close the gates of a city. Neither did they have the authority to mobilize the militia against the enemy. Their job was simply to communicate what they saw to those who did have the authority. Presently, most pastors or elders are trying to do this job for their congregations, which only distracts them from their own calling. We must begin to recognize, train and properly position those who have this calling, making sure that we establish and maintain clear lines of communication with them.

It is understandable why many leaders are both wary and weary of those who claim to be watchmen. Many who claim this position are just fearful or suspicious people who have assumed an office to which they have not been called. Many others genuinely have the calling, but try to use their gifts to usurp the authority of the elders to dictate policy or actions. Trust is the bridge that makes a relationship possible. Without it, there cannot be a genuine, effective relationship. Until trust is established between the elders and the watchmen, they will not be able to function together as they are called.

Many leaders are so wounded and worn out from the ministries of those who presumed to be watchmen or prophets that they do not want any more to do with such ministries. Likewise, many watchmen have been so wounded by pastors that they have lost their trust in the leadership of the church. There is usually a lot to overcome on both sides, but those who have a true vision of the Lord's purposes will overcome this barrier. We have no choice if we are going to walk in the unity that both the Lord and the times require. It will not be easy for either side to rebuild the bridge of trust, but it will be worth it.

The pastors and elders will never be able to function on the level of authority that they are called to until the watchmen are functioning properly. But let us understand that the trust required on both sides is something that only comes with faithfulness—we must never give up on each other. Every relationship is tested, and the greater the tests that we endure, the stronger the relationship will ultimately be. Until the relationship between leaders and watchman is reestablished properly, the watchmen cannot function and the leaders will continue to be needlessly blind-sided by the enemy.

Paul talked about how careful he was to stay within the realm of authority that had been appointed to him (II Corinthians 10:12-14). He knew that if he got outside of the limits God had set for him he would be vulnerable to the enemy. Leaders must allow the watchmen to function as God intends, and watchmen must learn that it is their job only to transmit information, not to dictate policy. Likewise, watchmen who are appointed to patrol out in the world (studying cults, political or philosophical trends, etc.) will become a stumbling block if they also try to watch over what is going on inside the church. And those who are called to watch over the church usually develop an unhealthy paranoia when they start trying to see what is going on out in the world.

Although it is often hard to stay within our realm of authority, when we do not do so, the consequences will almost always be destructive. In order to work together harmoniously, we will need to recognize when we have been operating outside the sphere of authority God has given to us. Then we can transfer some of the burdens we are now bearing to those who are in the proper sphere of authority to handle such matters.

Some Practical Applications

I have witnessed many practical applications of the watchman aspect of the prophetic ministry. One example of this occurred at a conference where I was speaking. One of the prophetic men from the congregation sponsoring the conference had a dream giving the name of a man who would come to the conference and seek to perpetuate an agenda that was not the Lord's. The registrations were checked and, sure enough, this man's name was on it (he was previously unknown to the prophet or to the leaders of this church). The man did indeed come seeking an audience with the leaders, and he had an agenda that would have been a major diversion for this congregation. The dream of one prophetic "watchman" possibly avoided years of frustration for this church.

In our local congregation we are placing those with the gift of discernment with the ushers and with the home group leaders. They are not there to be suspicious of people;

instead, they are to first discern what the Lord is doing, and then be quick to recognize the enemy's attempts to thwart that purpose. We are a young congregation, but already this has saved us from some very long-term problems that would have resulted if the enemy had been able to gain a foothold, or maybe even build a stronghold, in certain ministries within the church. We are especially concerned that watchmen be placed in the children's and youth ministries, for we know that the enemy is unleashing a major onslaught against the coming generation because of the Lord's mighty destiny for them.

Serving as spiritual watchmen will be one of the primary functions of the emerging prophetic ministry in the body of Christ. This will be on all levels, with some assigned to local congregations and ministries, and others serving on a national or international level. As these watchman ministries become more mature and dependable, we will seldom be needlessly blind-sided by the enemy again. We will be prepared for his assaults and will turn them back. Sometimes we will even set ambushes for him! This alone can have a major impact on the effectiveness of the entire church.

As watchmen become effective, a huge burden can be lifted from the leadership of the church. Leaders will be able to focus more on what they are truly called to do, and great spiritual advances will be the result. However, if we are called to this watchman ministry, let us be patient in waiting for our placement in the body of Christ. If we have a true gift, and manifest the fruit of the Spirit, our gift will make a place for us.

Our primary goal must always be first to gain the endorsement of God, not men. If we want the endorsement of God, we must be devoted to truth, integrity and submission to His Spirit. If it takes others a while to acknowledge our calling, we can give ourselves to growing in grace and discernment while we are waiting. **"For if the bugle produces an indistinct sound, who will prepare himself for battle?" (I Corinthians 14:8)** When you can produce a distinct sound, the church will hear you.

Bringing Correction

We must also understand that the watchman ministry was not given to bring correction to the church—that is one of the functions of the elders. Watchmen are called to give accurate information to the elders and then trust and support what is done with that information. The Old Covenant prophetic ministry was often used to bring correction, but usually the correction was spoken to the kings or elders. However, we do not see the New Covenant prophets being used nearly as much in that way, as this duty was assumed more by the apostles and elders.

If we are called to bring correction, we must follow the biblical procedures, such as those outlined in Matthew 18:15-17. If the Lord shows us something that is wrong in a person's life, our first response must be to go to that person in private. If He shows us something that is wrong in a congregation, we must take it in private to those who have been given responsibility for that congregation. I have witnessed several tragic mistakes made in giving words of correction openly in an assembly, but I have never seen one instance when I thought such a rebuke was from the Lord.

The Lord used a word of knowledge to bring correction to the woman at the well (John 4). We should learn from the great wisdom and gentleness with which He did this. The Lord's correction of this one woman resulted in the entire city being opened to the gospel, which probably set the stage for Philip's later visit and the remarkable revival in that region. Whenever we bring correction, we must always remember that we are correcting someone else's children—the Lord's!

The Old Covenant prophets often did bring correction harshly, but they were a reflection of the covenant under which they operated—the Law, which was harsh and unyielding. We are now under the age of grace, and the New Covenant prophet should reflect the nature of this covenant under which he is operating. As the Lord so clearly modeled for us, correction now comes with grace, which brings not only forgiveness but also the empowerment to be freed from the sin. Grace also imparts a prophetic vision of the promises of God for those who walk in obedience. We must always minister with the truth that sets people free (John 8:32).

The importance of the "watchman" aspect of the prophetic ministry is itself worthy of an entire book, which will be coming later. This is an important aspect of the prophetic that must be restored to the church, and it is presently one of the most distorted and abused. We are devoted to seeing it functioning with maturity and wisdom in our own congregation and ministry before we have much more to say about it.

SEVENTEEN

Words Of Life

Death and life are in the power of the tongue,
And those who love it will eat its fruit (Proverbs 18:21).

Words have power. In a basic way, the very definition of life might be *communication.* The higher life forms in the animal kingdom are considered to be those that can *communicate* on a higher level. To communicate means "to exchange." We determine that something is alive as long as it is able to communicate or interact with its environment, such as breathing the air or partaking of food. When this exchange stops, death has come.

Jesus said, **"The words that I have spoken to you are** *spirit and are life"* **(John 6:63).** We have true spiritual life to the degree that our communication with the Lord is developed and maintained. If we have spiritual communication with Jesus, people can kill our body but they cannot kill us, because our life is on a higher level.

211

Jesus is the Word of God (John 1:1). He is the Father's communication with the creation. Those who hear His voice are joined to the greatest power in the universe—the power of life. One word from the Lord, and the creation was formed. The Lord did not bring forth the creation by *thinking*—He spoke. Likewise, the Lord did not instruct His disciples, "*Think* and this mountain will be moved," but rather **"Whoever *says* to this mountain..." (Mark 11:23).** Words are the conduit for the greatest power in the universe. The more spiritual we become, the more we will understand this.

The more closely joined we become to the Word Himself, the more precious and powerful our words will become. As someone once said, "It is amazing how few words the Word Himself used." The more valuable a thing is to us, the more carefully we will handle it. In the same way, we will be more careful with words as we grow in our comprehension of their power. And the more careful we are with this great power, the more power the Lord can entrust to us.

Timing

> **Like apples of gold in settings of silver is a word spoken in *right circumstances* (Proverbs 25:11).**

Words **"spoken in right circumstances"** are words that fit perfectly with those circumstances. Words that are spoken out of time can lose their power. Since the Lord moves in perfect order, *the anointing is often connected to timing.* If we are going to be used to speak His words, we must be sensitive not only to *what* He wants to say, but also to *when* He wants to say it.

Jesus' whole life on earth was a testimony to the grace of timing. He not only knew exactly *what* to say in every circumstance, He knew *when* to say it. He knew that a gentle teaching on living waters would touch the heart of the woman at the well, who was obviously living a life of discontent (see John 4). Jesus also knew that the teaching on being born again would capture the attention of Nicodemus (see John 3). Had those teachings been given in the opposite settings, they would probably not have had the impact that they did.

What the Lord is anointing for one person or group may not be what He is anointing for another. Even though the seven churches in Revelation all lived at the same time and in the same geographic location, they all needed a different prophetic word from the Lord (see Revelation 2 and 3). For our words to have the power that they are intended to have, we must abide in the Word Himself, for He is the language of the Spirit.

Transcending Human Language

In I Corinthians 2:6-16 Paul explained the importance of understanding and speaking spiritual words:

Yet we do speak wisdom among those who are
mature; a wisdom, however, not of this age, nor of the
rulers of this age, who are passing away;

but we speak God's wisdom in a mystery, the
hidden wisdom, which God predestined before the
ages to our glory;

the wisdom which none of the rulers of this age has
understood; for if they had understood it, they would
not have crucified the Lord of glory;

but just as it is written, "Things which eye has not
seen and ear has not heard, and which have not entered
the heart of man, all that God has prepared for those
who love Him."

For to us God revealed them through the Spirit; for
the Spirit searches all things, even the depths of God.

For who among men knows the thoughts of a man
except the spirit of the man, which is in him? Even
so the thoughts of God no one knows except the Spirit
of God.

Now we have received, not the spirit of the world, but
the Spirit who is from God, that we might know the
things freely given to us by God,

which things we also speak, not in words taught by
human wisdom, but in those taught by the Spirit,
combining spiritual thoughts with spiritual words.

But a natural man does not accept the things of the Spirit of God; for they are foolishness to him, and he cannot understand them, because they are spiritually appraised.

But he who is spiritual appraises all things, yet he himself is appraised by no man.

For who has known the mind of the Lord, that he should instruct Him? But we have the mind of Christ (I Corinthians 2:6-16).

The language of the Spirit transcends human language. It is contrary and offensive to the natural mind of men. This is one reason why the Lord speaks to us through dreams and visions. He is not trying to confuse us by all the strange symbols and metaphors that dreams and visions usually consist of, but He is trying to teach us the language of the Spirit—which is much greater than human language.

It has been said that "a picture is worth a thousand words." In the language of the Spirit, this is certainly true. The symbolism of dreams and visions often reveals far more than human language can. This is foolishness to the natural mind, but for those who are spiritual, it is a much higher form of communication.

Living waters come from the **"innermost being" (John 7:38-39).** To speak words of true life, we must share that which comes from our hearts, not just our minds. The Jewish exorcists in Acts 19:13-16 knew about Jesus in their minds, but He did not dwell in their hearts. Therefore, when they tried to use His name to drive out darkness, the darkness rose up and drove *them* out.

Demons are spiritual beings, and they only respond to words that are spiritual. For our words to have the power of light to drive out darkness, they must come from the heart, which is joined to the heart of God. We only have true spiritual authority to the degree that the King dwells within us.

We have probably all heard someone teach a message that they heard from someone else. Often the teaching was very anointed when the first person taught it, but devoid of anointing when repeated. That is because the one trying to repeat the teaching knew it in his mind, but had not yet had it transferred to his heart.

This does not mean that we cannot ever share something which was first given to another, for every time we share from the Scriptures we do that. But the words must become "ours." We cannot have a relationship with another person's knowledge of Jesus—He must be *our* Jesus. True ministry is not just parroting knowledge. True ministry is by the Spirit, who abides in our hearts. Only the Spirit can beget that which is spiritual (John 3:6).

And as for you, the anointing which you received from Him abides in you, and you have no need for

anyone to teach you; but as His anointing teaches you about all things, and is true and is not a lie, and just as it has taught you, you abide in Him (I John 2:27).

This scripture does not mean that we are not to receive teaching from people, for the Lord gave teachers to His church for that purpose. However, we must recognize the anointing of the Holy Spirit working through the people.

The men on the road to Emmaus were sensitive to the spiritual words spoken to them by Jesus because their hearts burned within them. However, they did not recognize the Lord until they saw Him break the bread. Our eyes will be opened when we see Jesus as the one who is breaking our bread and teaching us, regardless of through whom the teaching comes.

Walking in Truth

The great preacher, Charles Spurgeon, once lamented that he could find 10 men who would die for the Bible for every one who would read it. This ratio is probably accurate for other Christian duties as well. We can probably find 10 men who will fight for prayer in public schools for every one who actually prays with his children at home. We may have 10 men or women who complain about the sex and violence on television for every one who actually refuses to watch it. This must change. Our power to be salt and light in the world does not depend just on what we believe, but on our faithfulness to live our beliefs.

"That which is born of the flesh is flesh, and that which is born of the Spirit is spirit" (John 3:6). We are utterly dependent on the Holy Spirit for bearing true spiritual fruit. Because the Holy Spirit is **"the Spirit of truth" (John 16:13),** He will only endorse with His presence and power that which is true.

The Lord judges our hearts, not our minds. For this reason "heart religion" is about to take precedence over intellectual religion. However, we must never abandon our commitment to sound biblical truth. The highest levels of power will be given to those who have embraced both the Word and the Spirit. When we are abiding in the Lord, the Word and the Spirit are in perfect agreement.

The great darkness that is now sweeping the world has happened on our watch. The great release of power that is coming in Christian leadership will be the result of a deep repentance and conviction of sin that sweeps over the body of Christ. Movements that exhort men and women to fulfill their spiritual responsibilities will have a profound impact on the whole church. The repentance that resulted from the humiliations of the past decade is also about to bear great fruit.

As the Lord declared, **"Whoever exalts himself shall be humbled; and whoever humbles himself shall be exalted"** **(Matthew 23:12).** Even though much of the humility has been the result of God's judgment, the degree to which the church embraced the judgment has prepared her to be lifted up in the esteem of the nations. Even though the attacks and slander will always be with us, the world's esteem for the advancing church is about to rise dramatically.

The Patience for Lasting Fruit

Some consider it a travesty that the New Testament does not take a decisive stand against the great moral evils of the times in which it was written, such as slavery, abortion and infanticide. It is true that the first-century church leaders did not wage frontal assaults against these evils. However, it was not because of negligence or irresponsibility; instead, they had a higher strategy for using a greater power. They did not just flail at the branches of human depravity—they put the ax to the root of the tree.

With focused, unyielding concentration, the apostles of the early church maintained their frontal assault on sin. They drove back the spirit of death by lifting up the Prince of Life. When the issue of slavery did arise in his letter to Philemon, Paul did not attack the issue of slavery directly, but rose above it by appealing to love and the fact that the slave, Onesimus, was a Christian brother. This may offend the penchant for militancy that issue-oriented activists usually have, but it is the way of the Spirit. As even the secular historian, Will Durant, observed, "Caesar tried to change men by changing institutions. Christ changed institutions by changing men."

The way of the Spirit is to penetrate beyond what a frontal assault on issues can usually accomplish. There are times for bold confrontations, but usually the Lord works much more slowly than we are willing to accept. This is because He is working toward a much deeper, more complete, and lasting change. The Lord works from the inside out, not the outside in.

The **"divinely powerful"** weapons are about to be reclaimed and used on an unprecedented scale by the church (see II Corinthians 10:3-5). As intercessory and spiritual warfare movements continue to mature, the results will become increasingly spectacular. Even so, the most powerful weapon given to the church is *spiritual truth*. Facts can be "truth," but spiritual truth is only found when knowledge is properly combined with *life*. It is when we live what we believe that we embrace spiritual, eternal truth. As the church begins to live the truth that she knows, her light will increase and shine into the darkness.

Light is more powerful than darkness. Love is more powerful than hatred; life is more powerful than death. As we begin to walk in the light, the love and the life of the Son of

God, we will put darkness and death to flight. The power of the church lies not just in her ability to articulate the truth, but to walk in it. This is the foundation of the great release of power that is coming to the body of Christ.

The Greater Wisdom

The way of the Spirit is practical. He is working to have the will of God done on earth as it is in heaven (Matthew 6:10). We too must be committed to seeing practical fruit. However, our desire not to be "so heavenly minded that we are of no earthly good" has often resulted in our becoming so *earthly* minded that we are not doing any *spiritual* good. If we impact men spiritually, it will ultimately result in earthly good, but the reverse is not true. If we only impact institutions and outward behavior, we may change the facade of things, but we have not dealt with the roots and they will sprout again.

It is not just bearing fruit that counts, but bearing fruit that *remains* (John 15:16). In order to bear the fruit that is eternal, we must learn patience. We are exhorted to be **"imitators of those who through faith *and patience* inherit the promises" (Hebrews 6:12).** The great wisdom that is about to come upon the church is to see from the eternal perspective, which will impart the essential ability to plan with strategy and vision for lasting fruit.

The original apostolic burden—to labor until Christ was formed in His people and to present all men complete in

Christ (Galatians 4:19, Colossians 1:28)—is still the true burden of apostolic and prophetic ministries. We are called to be like Christ and to do the works that He did. When this is achieved, He will be so lifted up by His people that all men will be drawn to Him.

The Morning Star
PROPHETIC BULLETIN

In order to swiftly promulgate important, prophetic messages to the body of Christ, we have instituted this service. The primary contributors will be **Paul Cain, Bobby Conner, Bob Jones** and **Rick Joyner.** Other proven prophetic ministries will contribute at times. *Distribution will be at irregular times dictated by the timeliness and importance of the messages received.*

Only...$5.00!
for a 1 year subscription
Catalog No. MSPB-001
$7.00 USD for foreign subscriptions.

CALL 1-800-542-0278
———— TO ORDER ————
CREDIT CARD ORDERS ONLY.